Beginning Rock / Pop Guitar Etudes

by Adam Douglass

Online Video

Video
dv.melbay.com/30648
You Tube
www.melbay.com/30648V

I0805606

MEL BAY®

Visit us on the Web at www.melbay.com — E-mail us at email@melbay.com

Foreword

Etude, literally translated from French, means "study," but in the musical world it is more akin to an "exercise" addressing one or two specific techniques. In taking up most instruments, the student can easily find a massive number of etude books which provide complete musical pieces; when played start-to-finish, etudes generally sound like something whole, although they may not be aesthetically satisfying or match the student's musical tastes or aspirations.

For those interested in learning pop/rock-related guitar music, the task of finding appropriate etudes is even more daunting. Hours are spent daily on making the fingers faster and stronger while maintaining the proper arch and playing on the fingertips. Beginning guitar books offer little more than, "Here's a Beatles song. Good luck with the F♯m chord!" And yet, a certain musicality is lacking in endlessly toggling back and forth between the E, A, and D chords.

The purpose of this book is to bring musicality into the beginning stages of learning the guitar, while incorporating the basic techniques used in playing the pop/rock style. These etudes address common techniques used by every pop/rock guitar player and songwriter. They are arranged in a progressive manner, so that upon completion of the book, you will have the hand strength and agility to tackle the challenging chords used by the most advanced guitarists. In addition to standard notation and tablature, this book's companion online video will serve as a visual and audio guide to how these etudes should be played.

Most importantly, however, these etudes will make the student feel like they are truly making music. Mastering one of these exercises will give the student the ability and confidence to say to friends and family, "Listen to this piece I've been practicing," or perhaps help them avoid the embarrassment of walking into a guitar shop to purchase a new instrument without have a complete pop/rock song to play.

The single most important thing about learning music, more so than cultivating a good practice ethic, is to enjoy oneself. That, in and of itself, is the seed that makes the promising beginner want to become an accomplished musician. For the novice student who has never played the guitar in his or her life, I strongly recommend that you find a competent teacher who can guide you in the use of the fundamental techniques used in these etudes. For the more experienced beginner, or someone who already plays another instrument, I hope these exercises will provide an enjoyable challenge for analysis, practice and use in creating rock/pop music of your own.

Most importantly, enjoy!
Adam W. Douglass

Dedication

I dedicate this book to my amazing wife, Jinnifer whose support, encouragement and computer wizardry made it all possible.

Contents

Key

X - When used in a chord grid or diagram, means "Don't play this note."

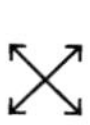 - Mute or "damp" this note with a finger from an adjoining string; allow the resulting "thunk" to sound as a rhythmic element. As shown on page 19.

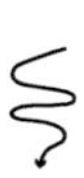 - Strum the chord broadly, proportionate to the tempo of the piece.

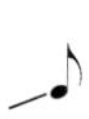 - Slide or glisssando upward. As show on page 21.

harm. - Indicates "harmonics" which could be natural or artificial.

Chord - Three or more tones sounded simultaneously.

Interval - The distance between two pitches sounded together (harmonic) or separately (melodic). Two notes do not form a chord.

¢ - Indicates ½ barre chord. As shown on page 9.

D.C. - Da Capo "from the top/head." Go back to beginning. As shown on page 11.

⑤ - Circle numbers represent specific strings where notes are played.

N.C. - "No Chord," possibly a campanella or "bell-like" melodic or arpeggio effect easily represented in a chord grid with open and stopped strings, but defying chord naming.

1

Power Ballad Etude

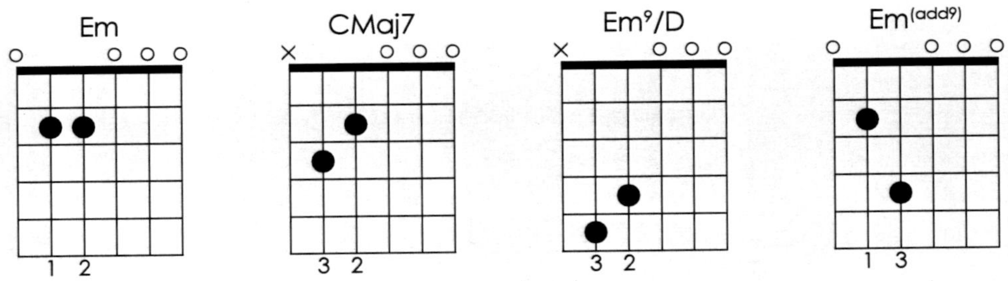

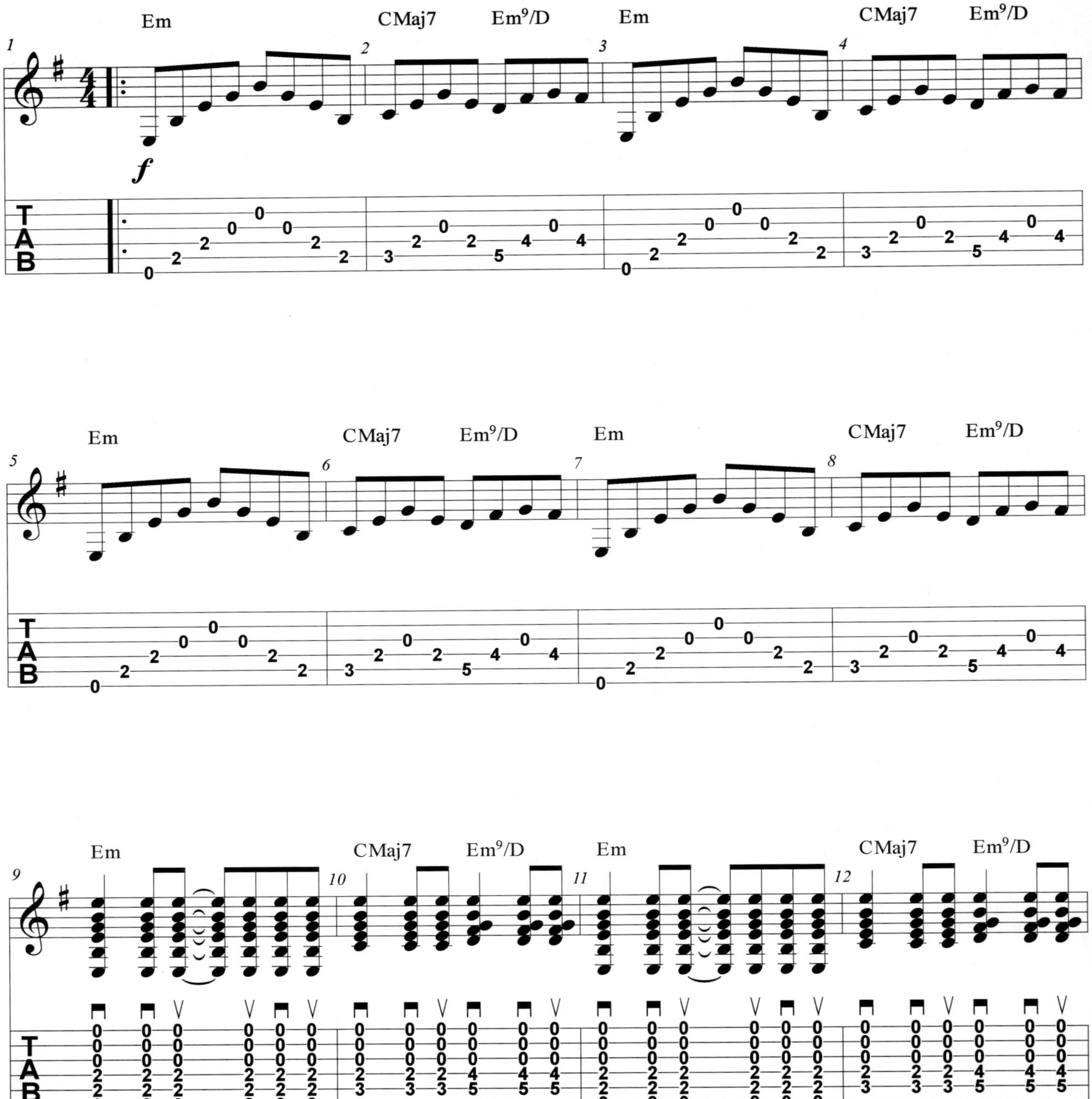

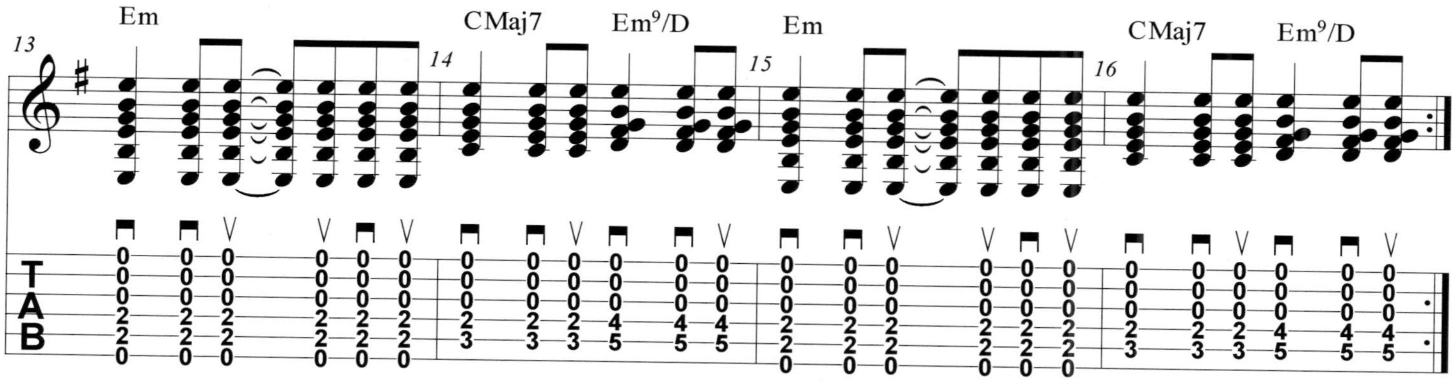
Em
CMaj7
Em9/D
Em
CMaj7
Em9/D
TAB

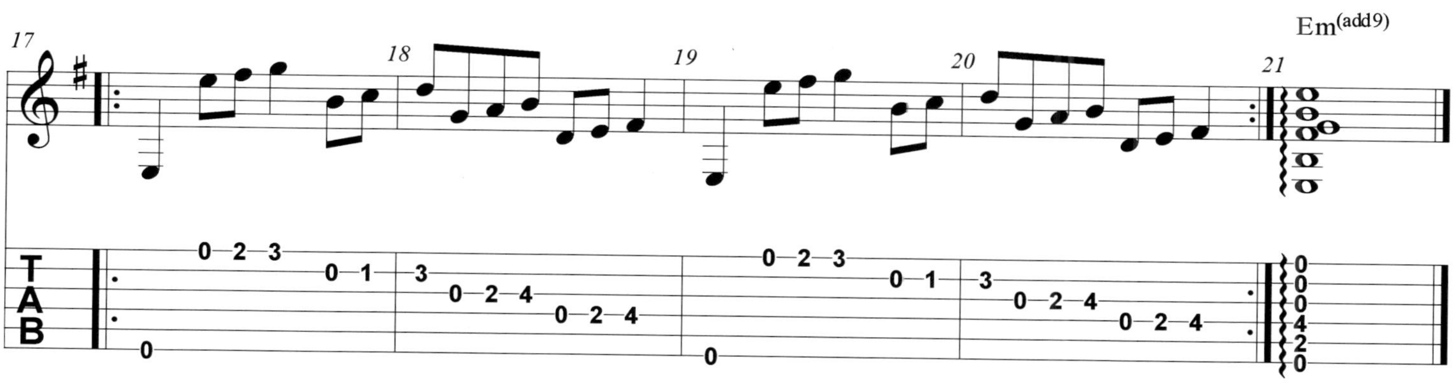
Em(add9)
TAB

2

90's Acoustic Rock Etude

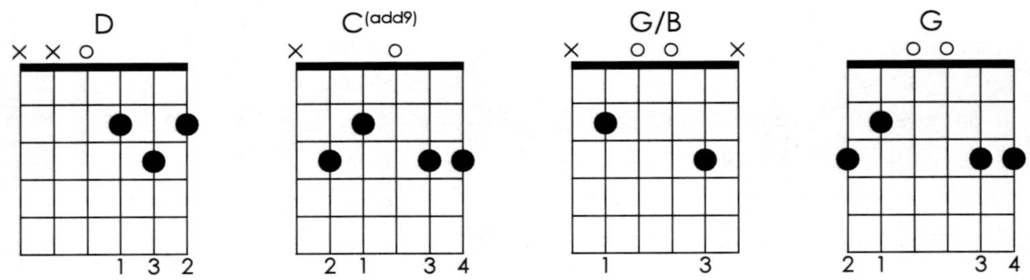

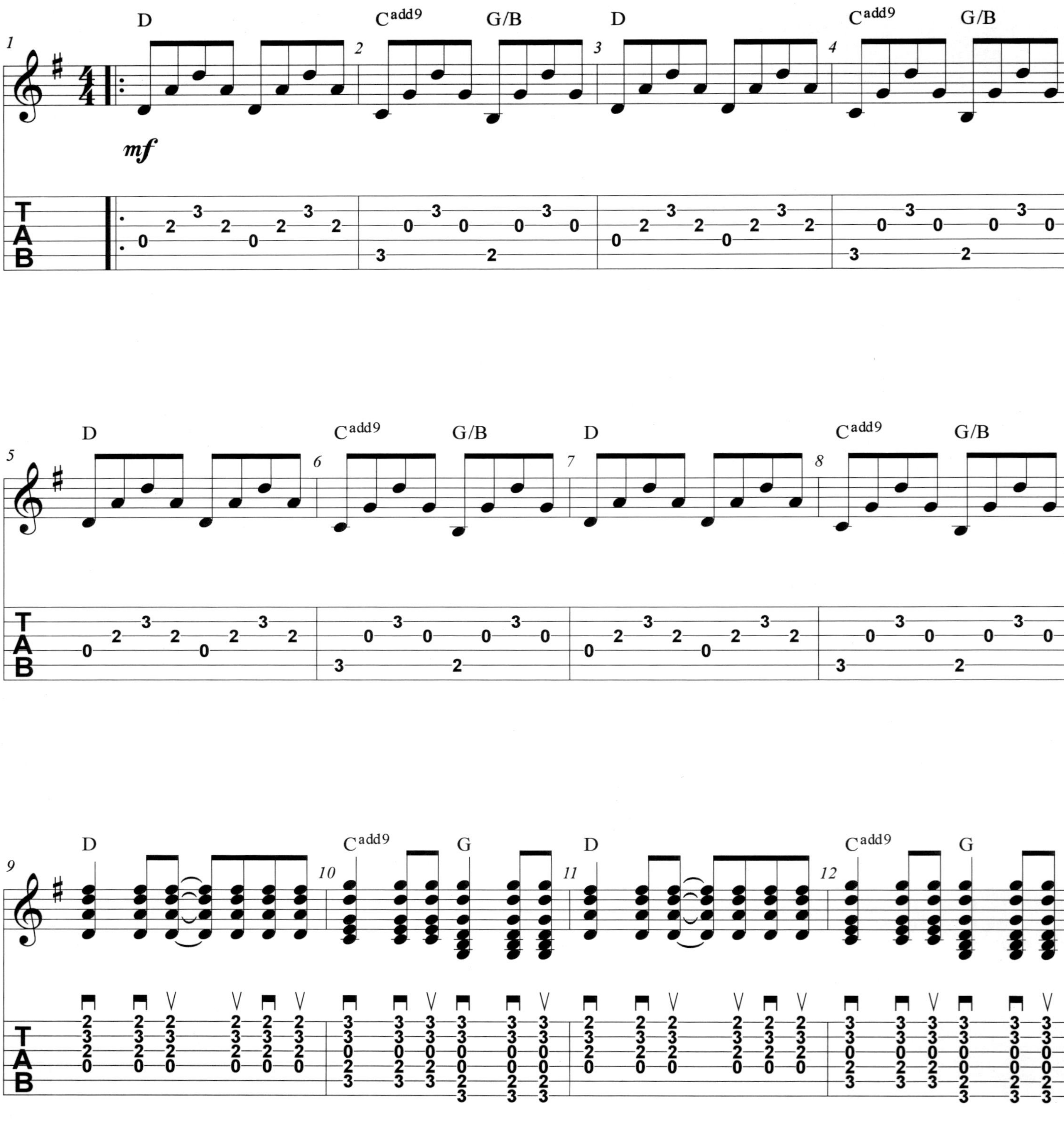

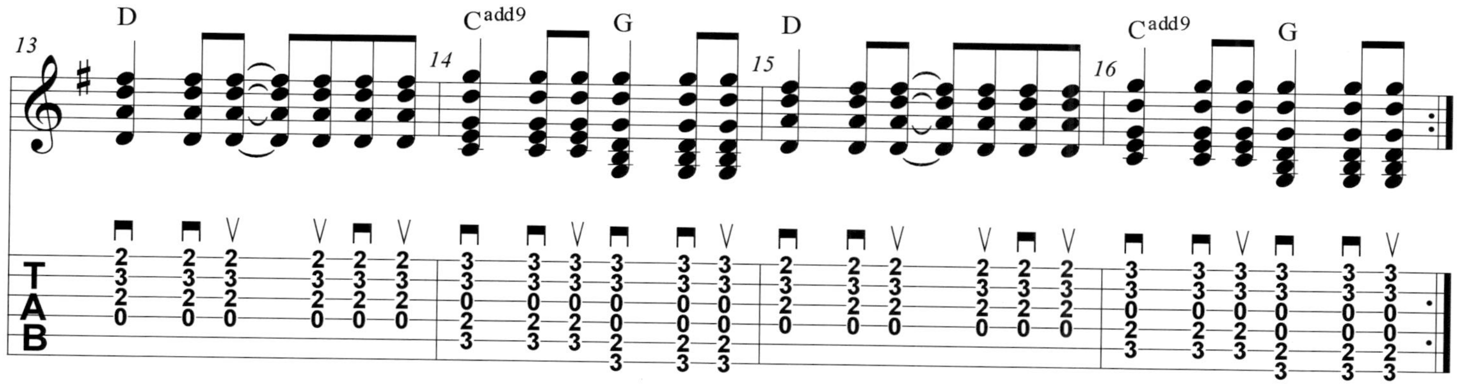

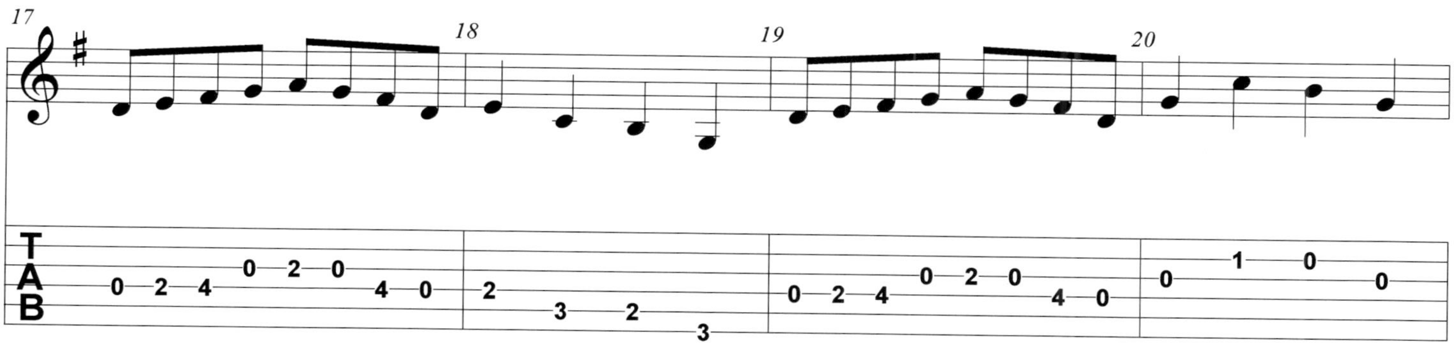

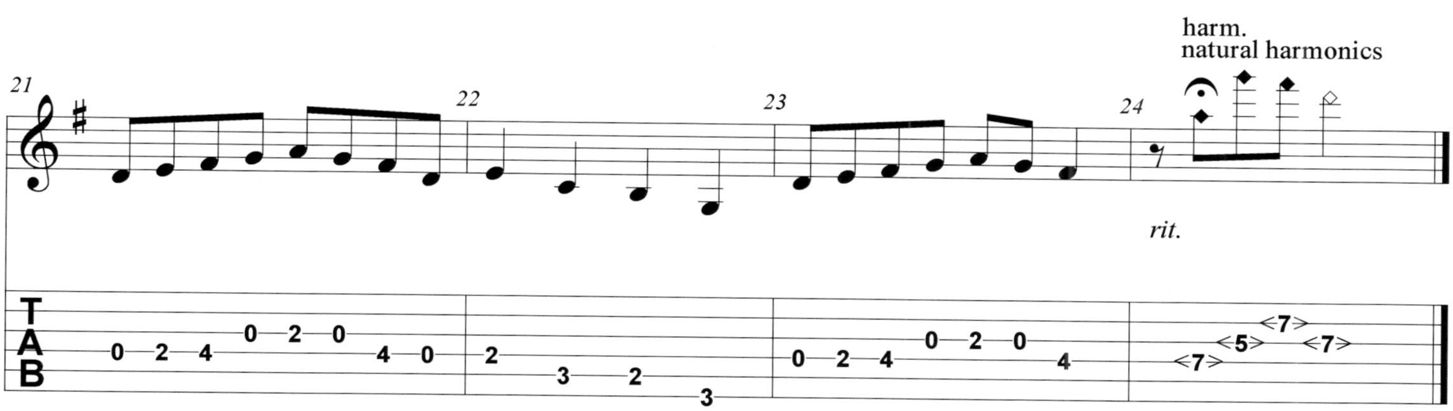

Natural Harmonics

Played by lightly touching the string directly over the indicated fret, and then plucking hard with the pick, closer to the bridge than usual. Allow the plucked string to "bounce" your left-hand fingers off the string so the harmonic continues to sound. Natural Harmonics can be found at all equal divisions of the open string—1/2, 1/3, 1/4, and 1/8 at corresponding frets 12, 7, 5 and 4 respectively.

Artificial Harmonics

Artificial Harmonics can be found 12 frets higher than any "stopped' or fingered left-hand note. Touch the string with the right-hand index finger, and pluck with the pick using an alternative thumb/middle/ring-finger pick-hold. Using a combination of artificial and natural harmonics, entire melodies can be played.

3

Progressive Rock Etude

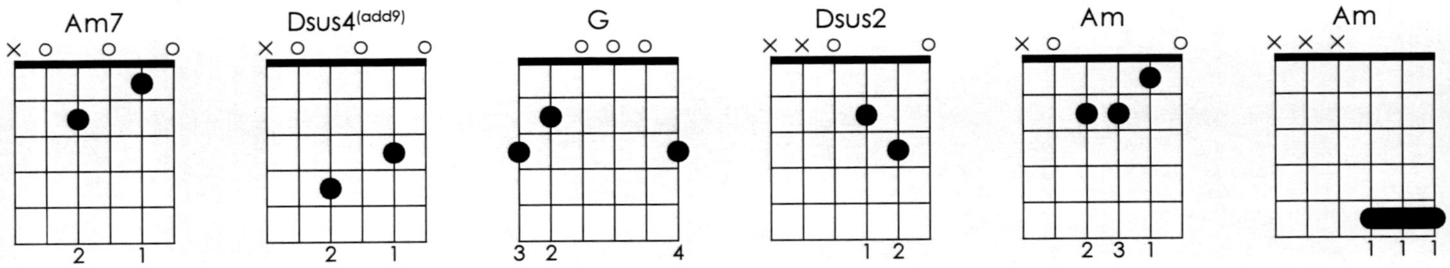

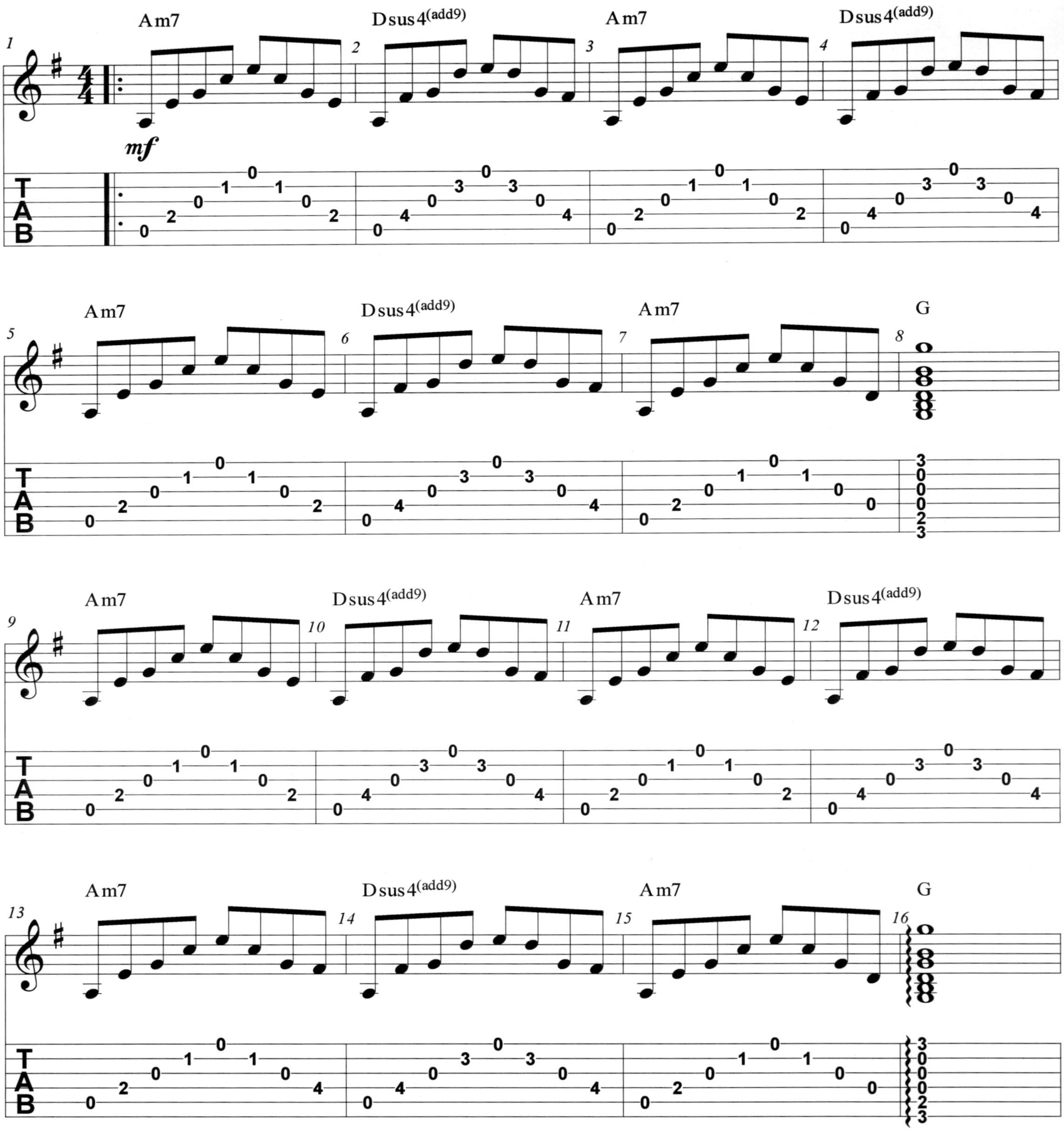

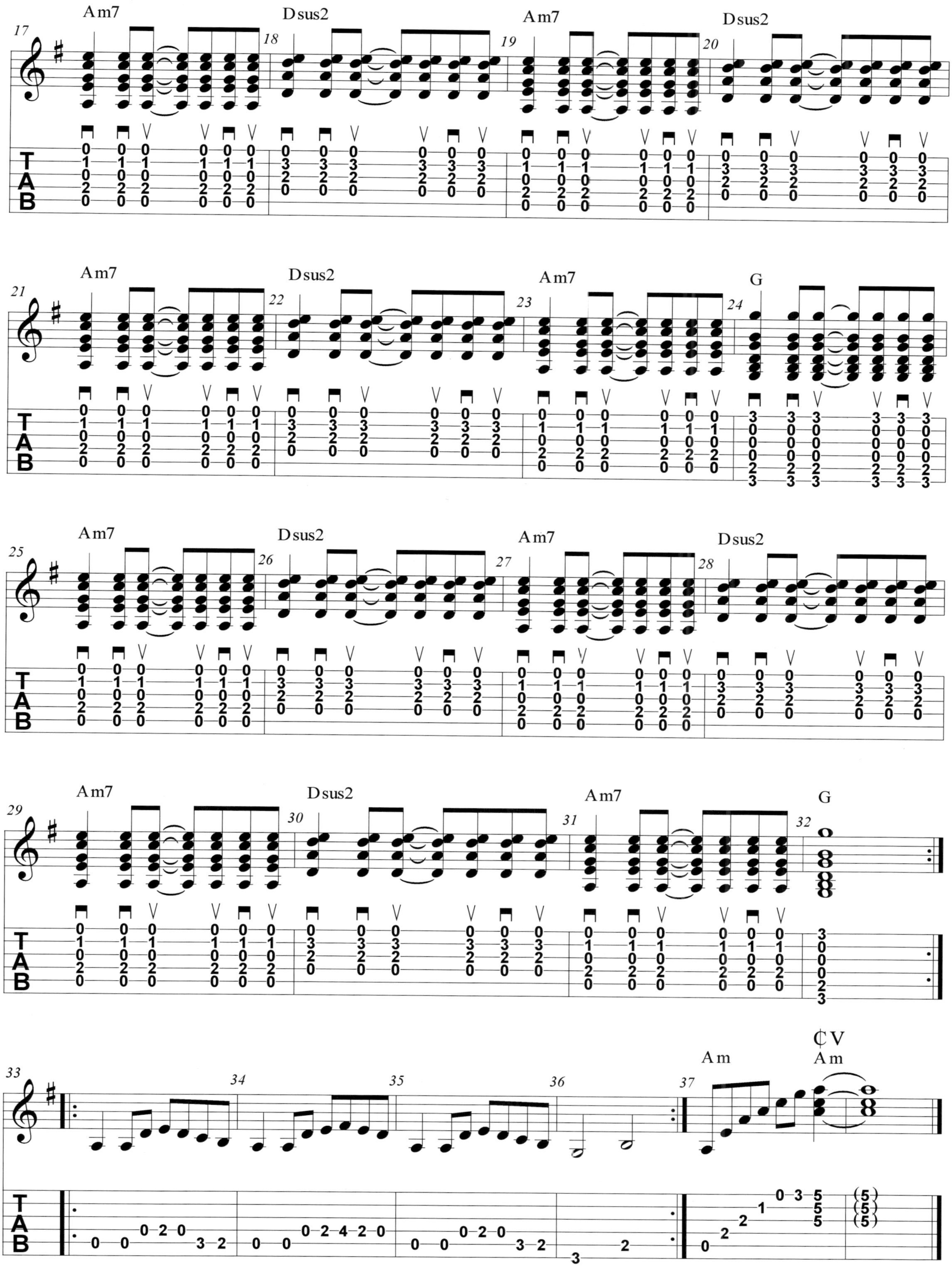
Am7
Dsus2
Am7
Dsus2
Am7
Dsus2
Am7
G
Am7
Dsus2
Am7
Dsus2
Am7
Dsus2
Am7
G
Am
CV
Am

4

Hard Rock Etude #1

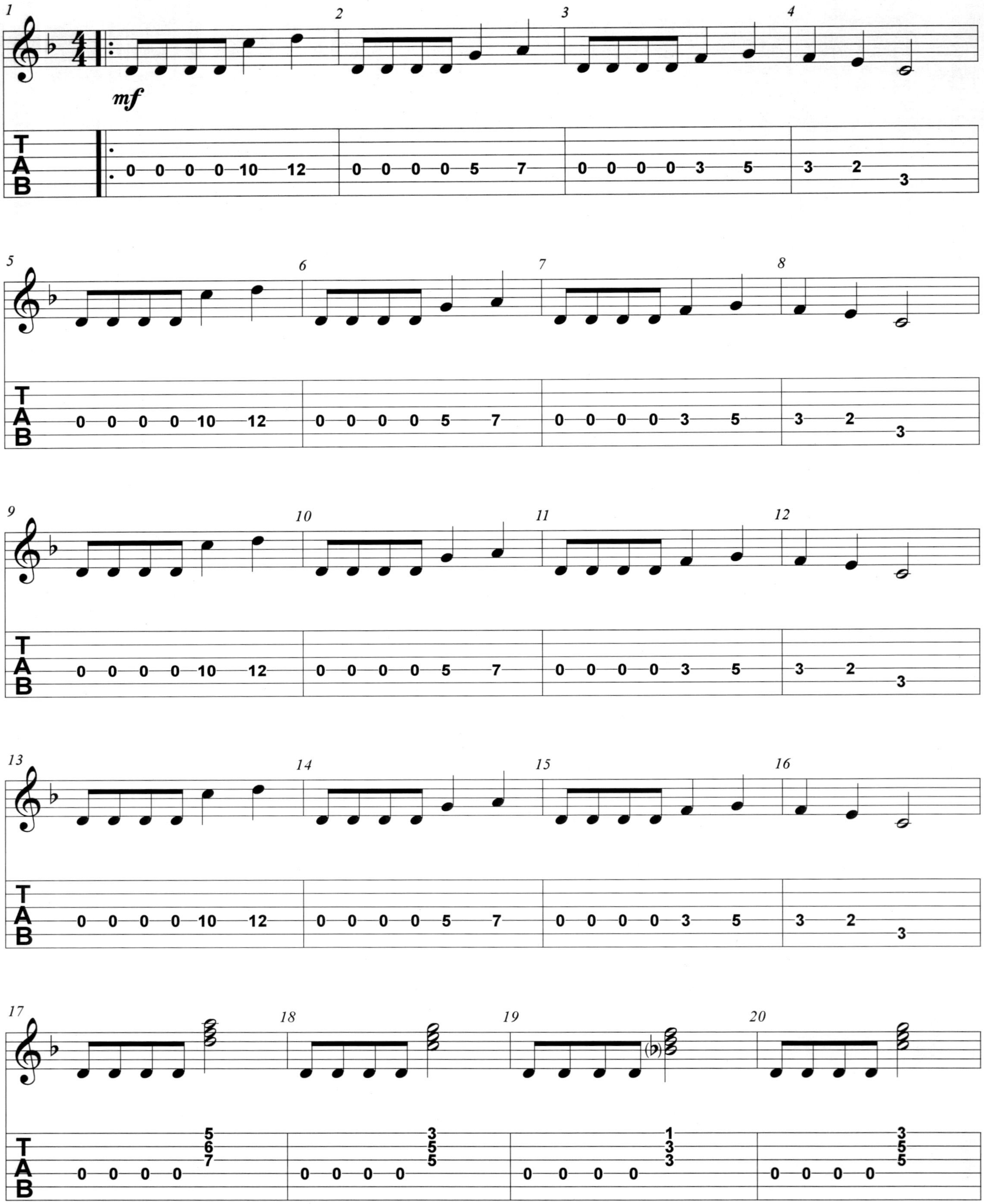

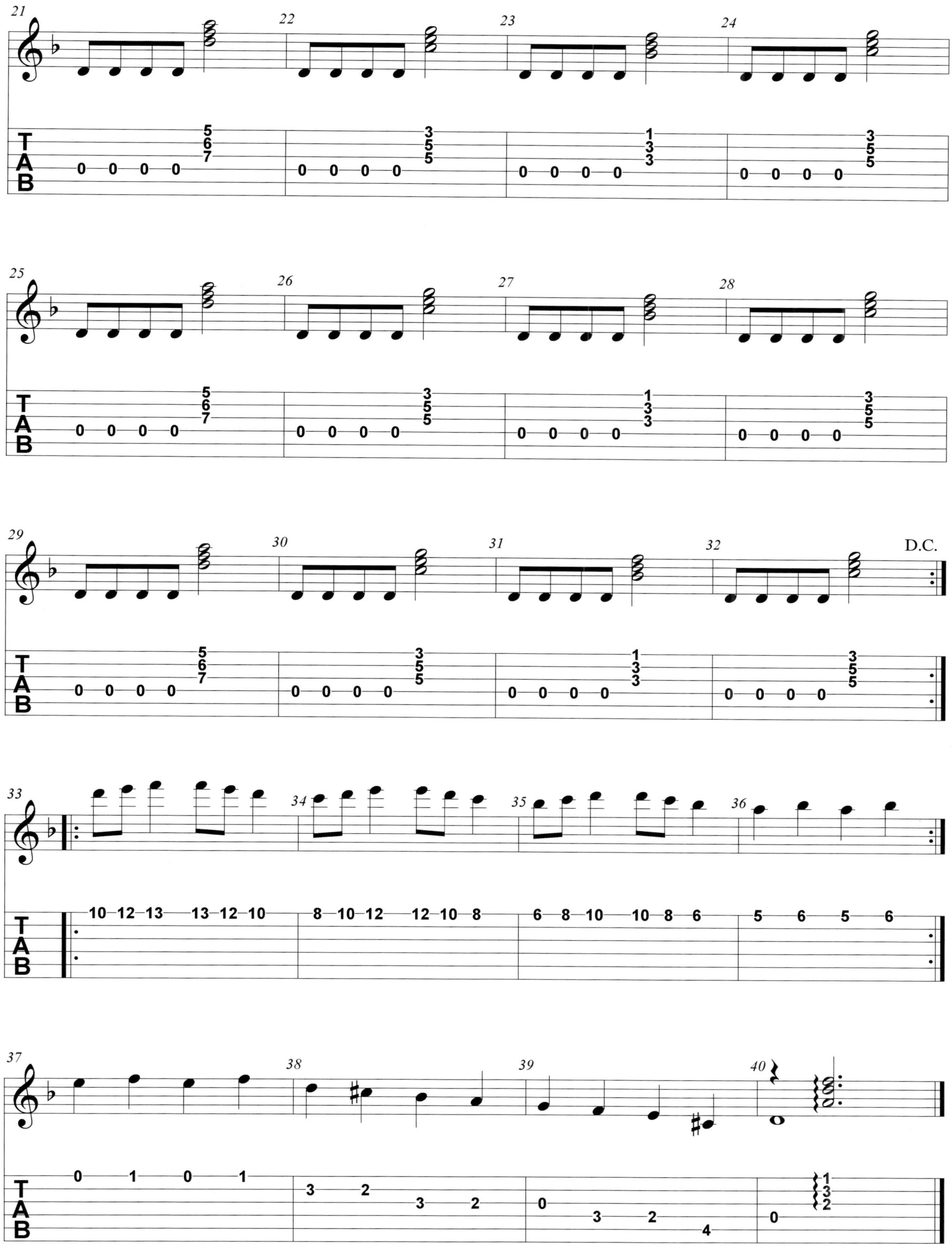
D.C.

5

Southern Rock Etude

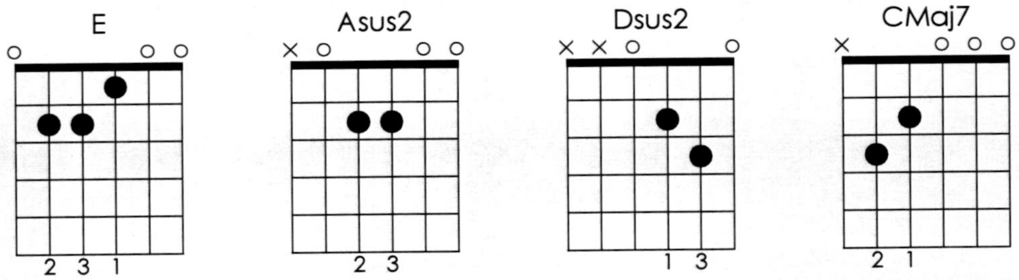

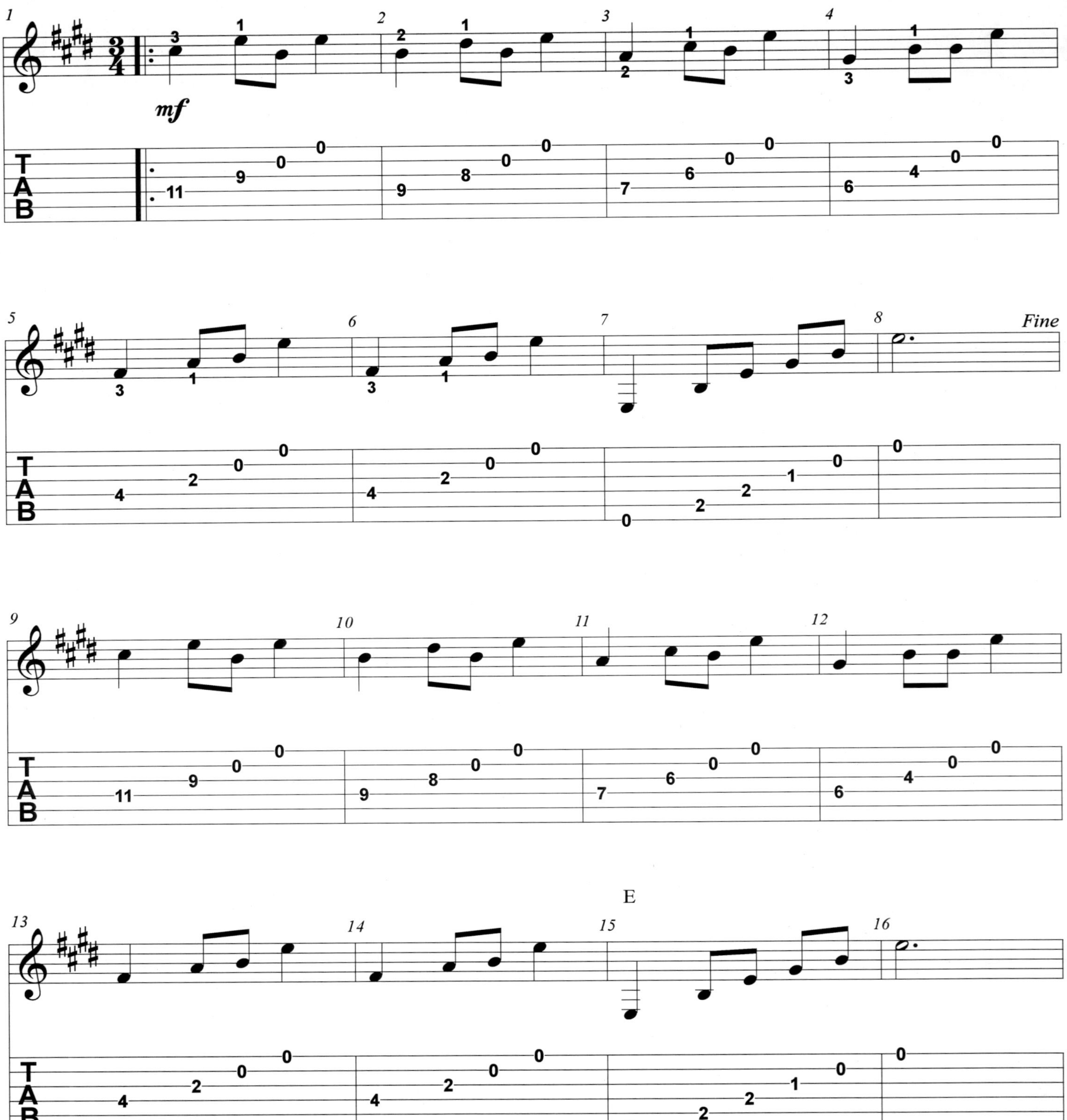

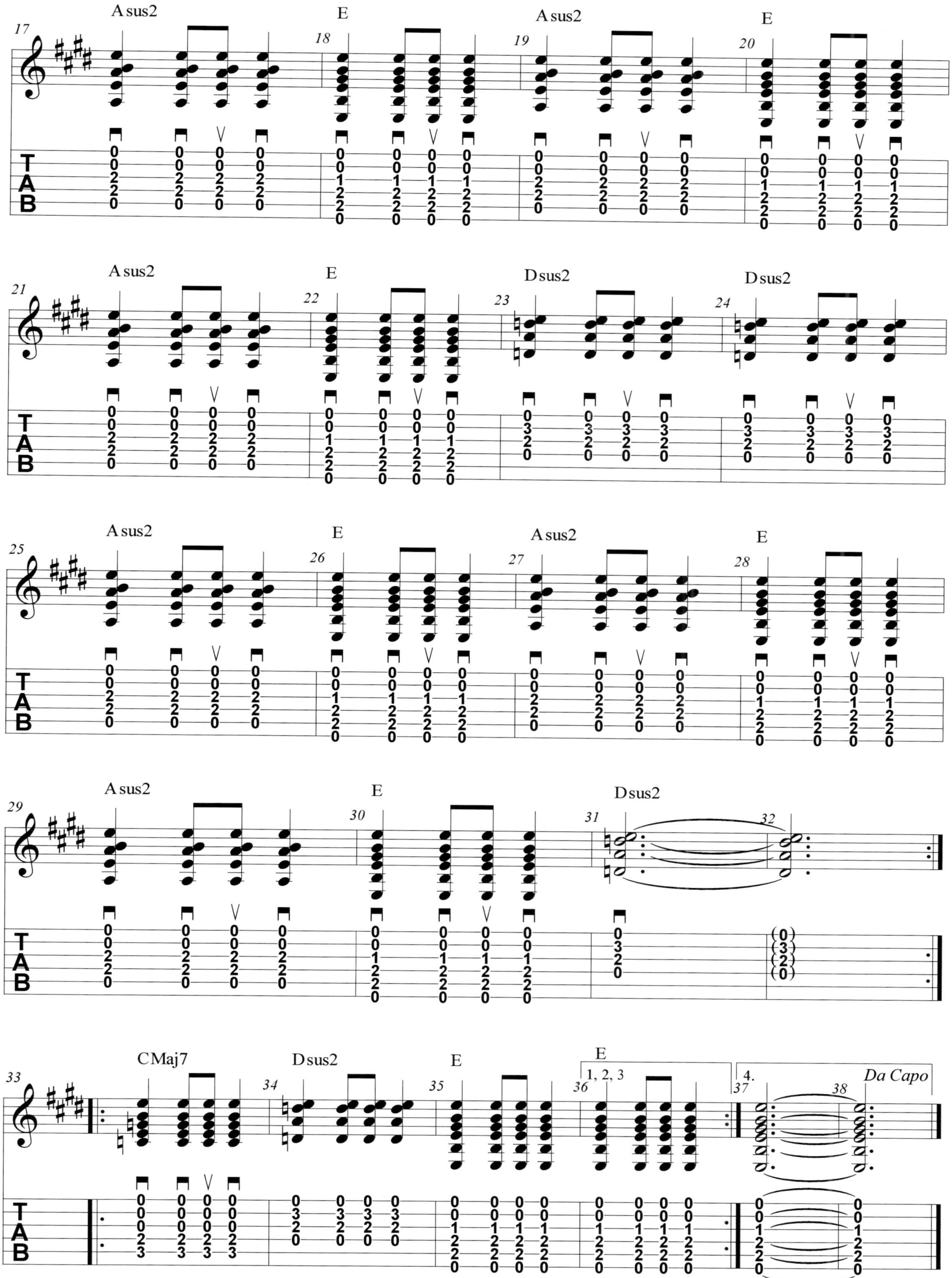
A sus2
E
A sus2
E
A sus2
E
D sus2
D sus2
A sus2
E
A sus2
E
A sus2
E
D sus2
CMaj7
D sus2
E
E
1, 2, 3
4.
Da Capo

6

Major / Minor Etude

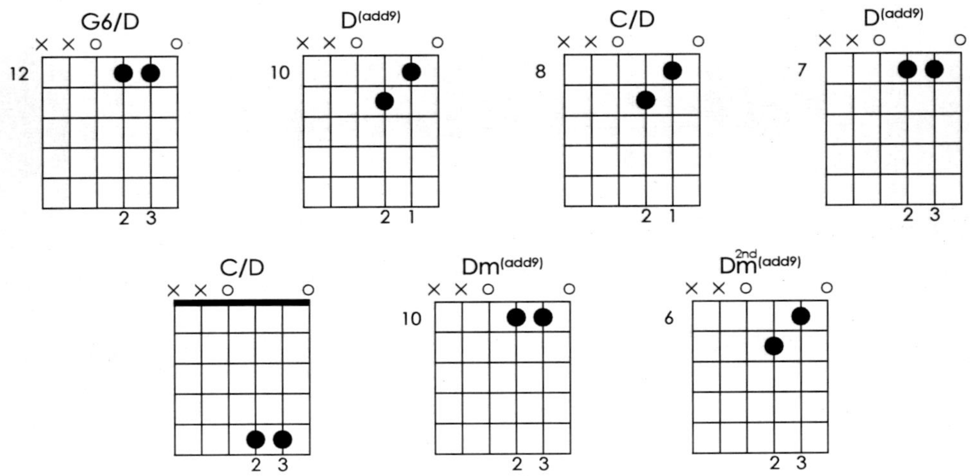

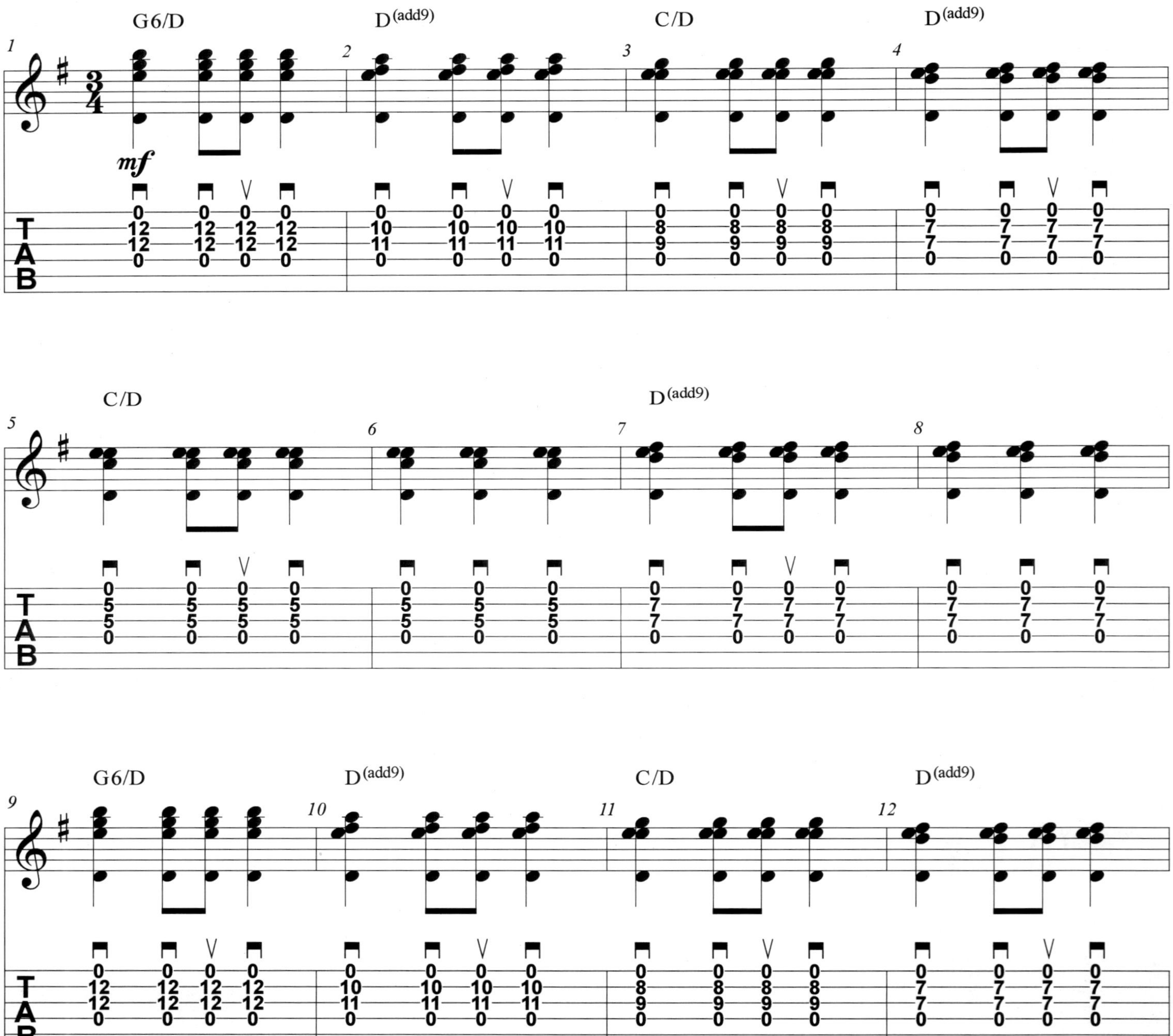

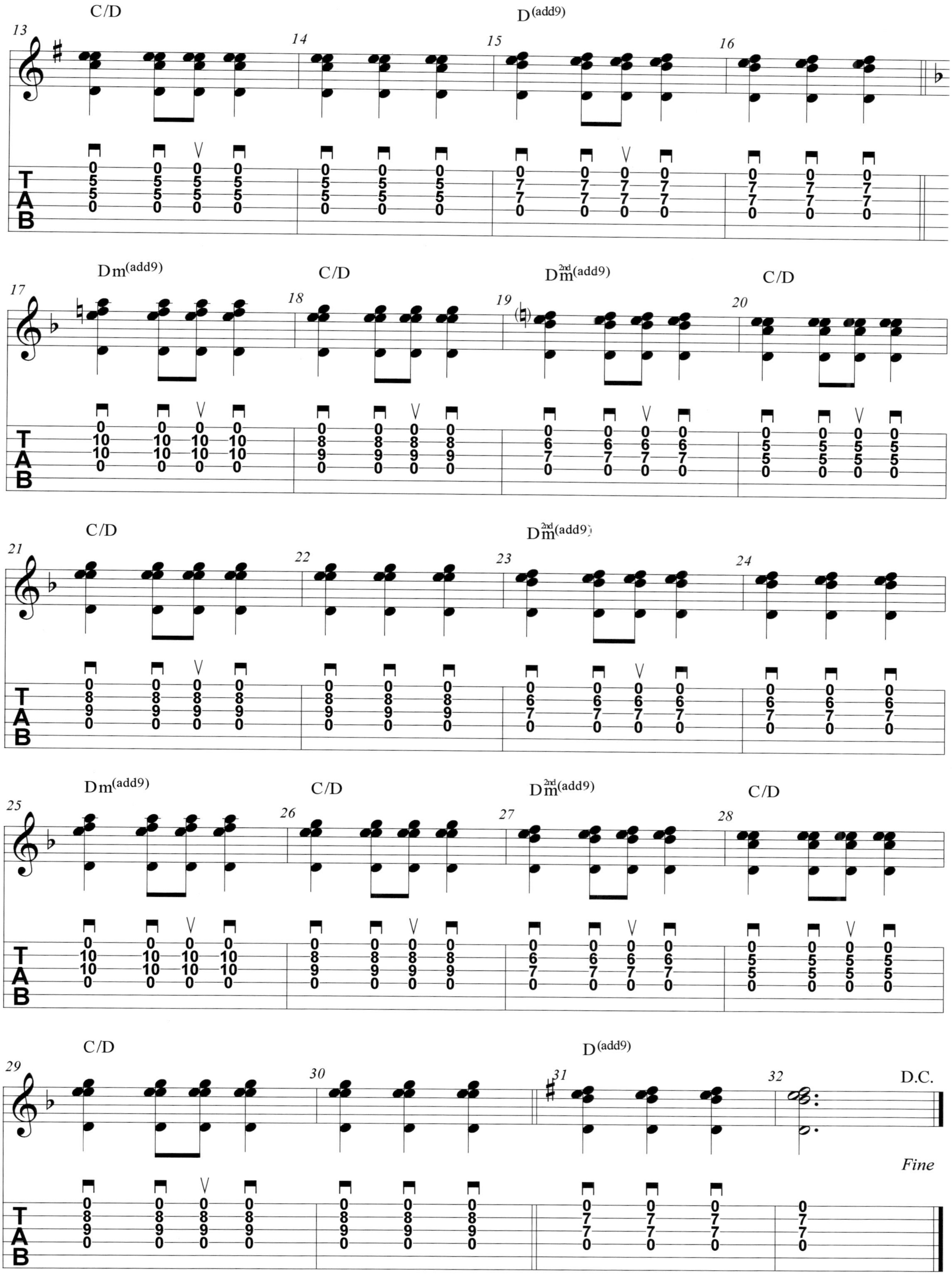
C/D
D(add9)
Dm(add9)
C/D
Dm2nd(add9)
C/D
C/D
Dm2nd(add9)
Dm(add9)
C/D
Dm2nd(add9)
C/D
C/D
D(add9)
D.C.
Fine

7

Pedal-Tone Etude

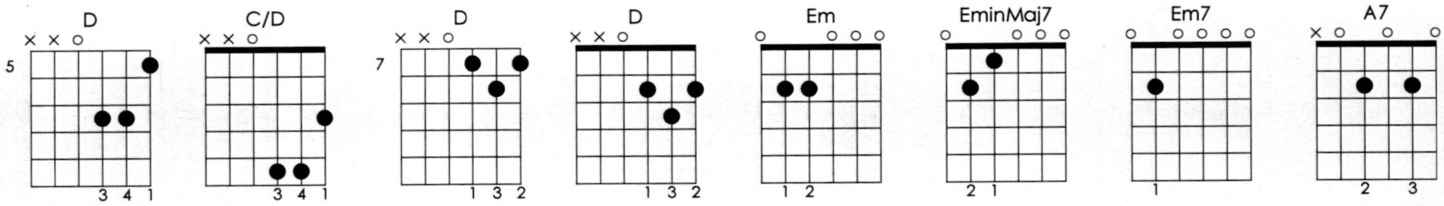

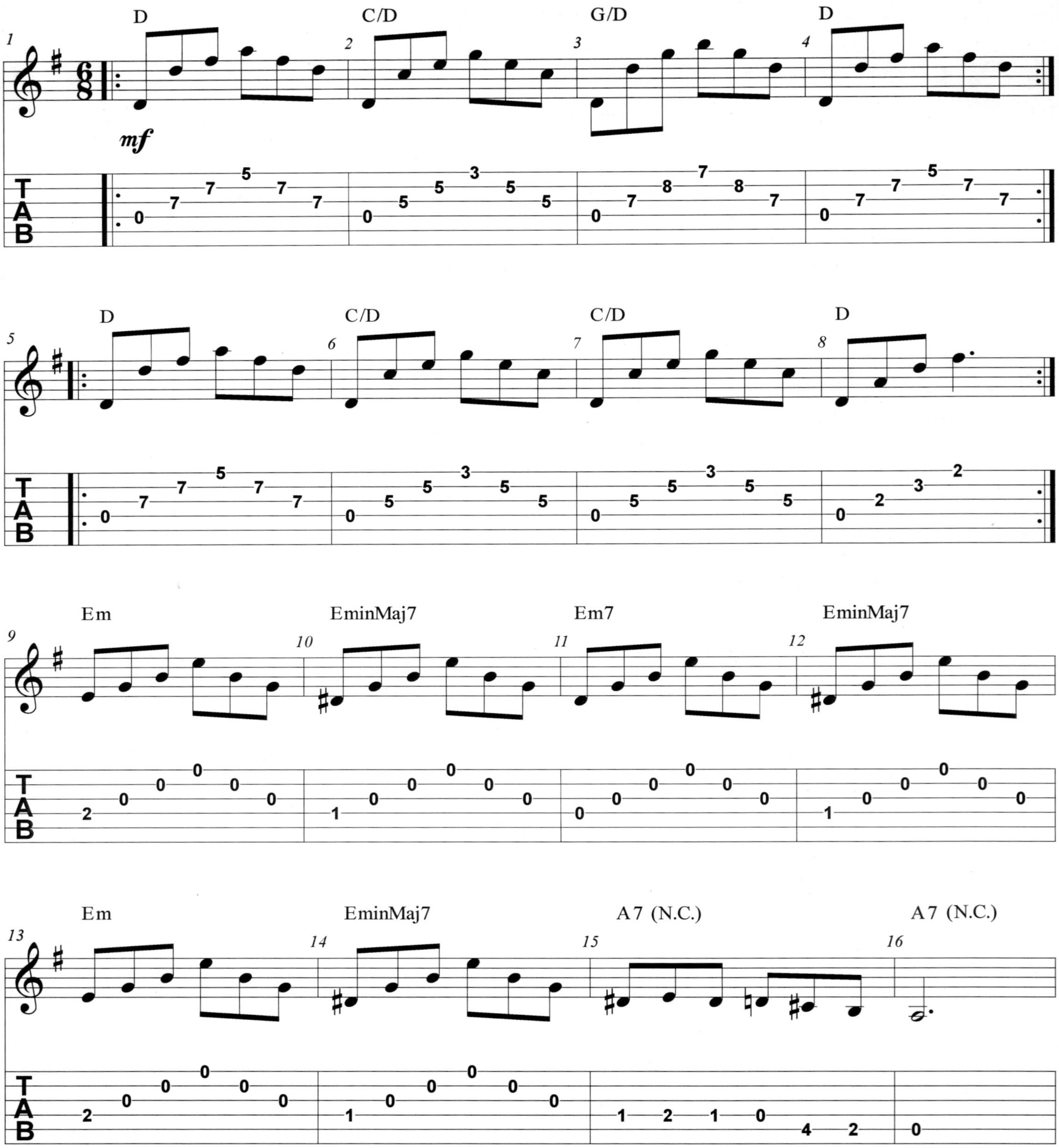

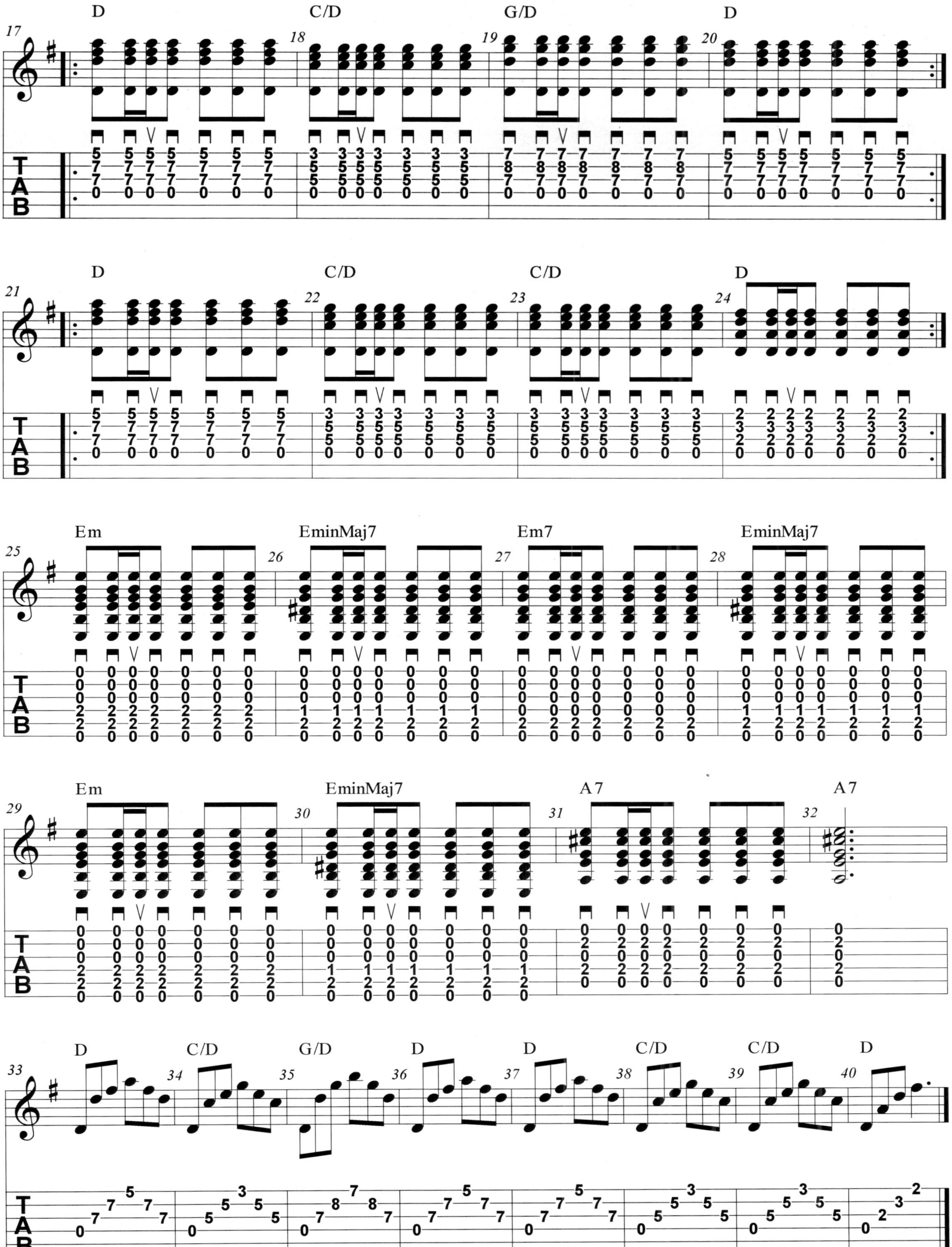
D
C/D
G/D
D
D
C/D
C/D
D
Em
EminMaj7
Em7
EminMaj7
Em
EminMaj7
A7
A7
D
C/D
G/D
D
D
C/D
C/D
D

8

Indie Rock Etude #1

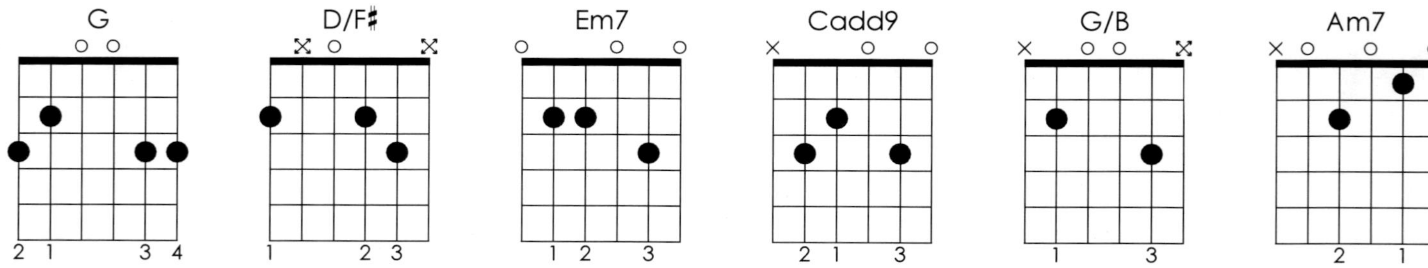

At measures 17 and 21,
⤧ = Damp (mute) unwanted non-chord tones.

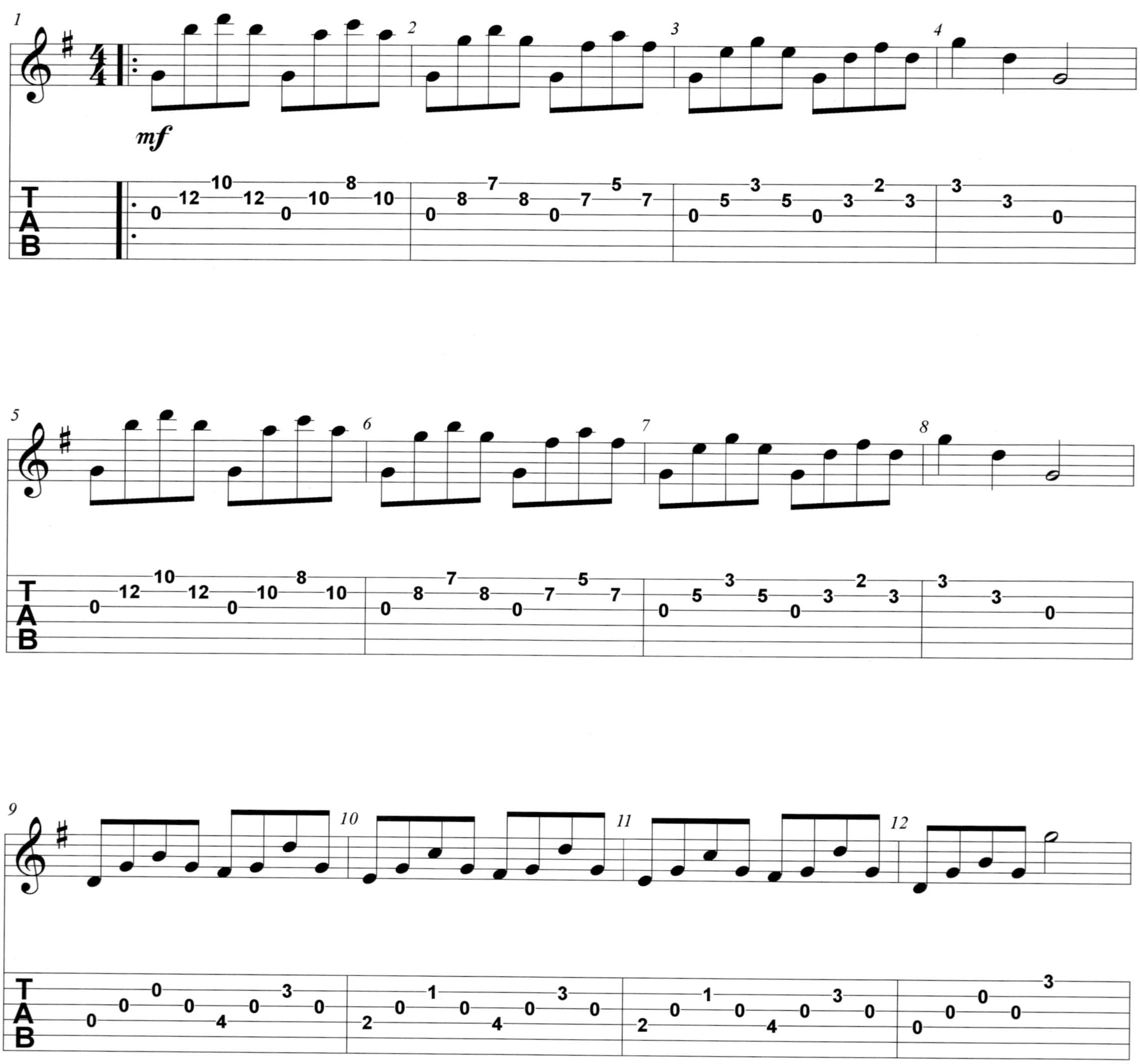

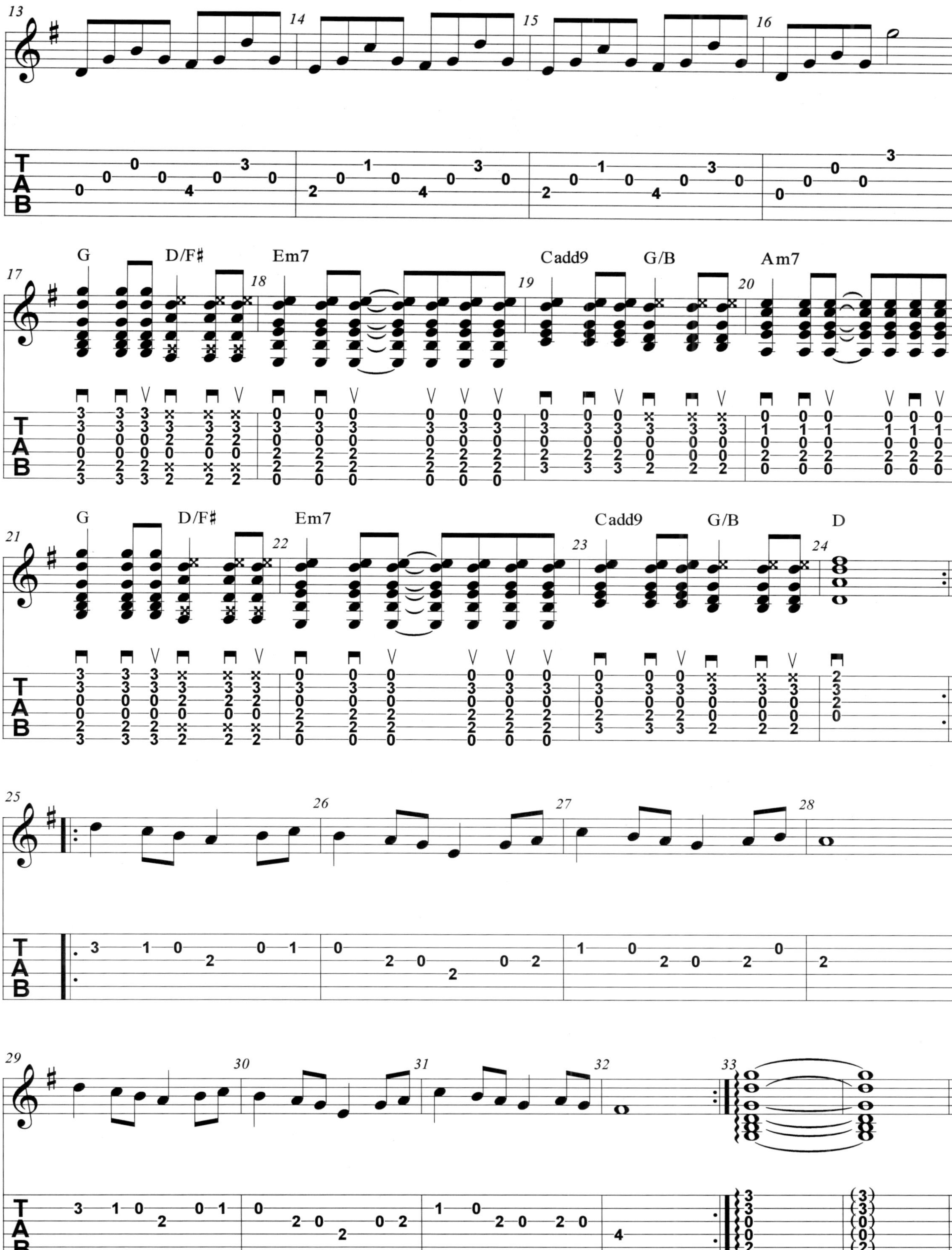
G
D/F♯
Em7
Cadd9
G/B
Am7
G
D/F♯
Em7
Cadd9
G/B
D

9

Indie Rock Etude #2

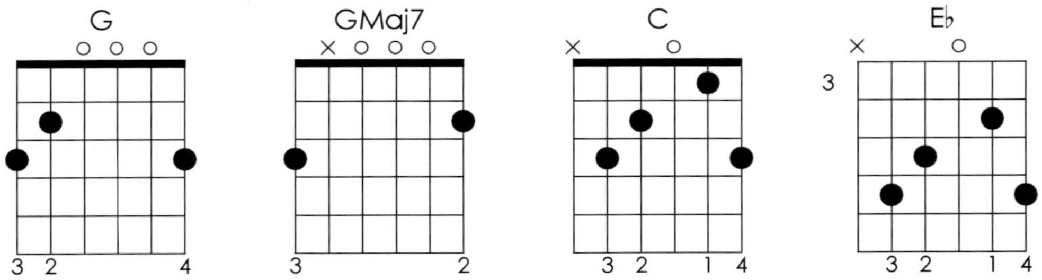

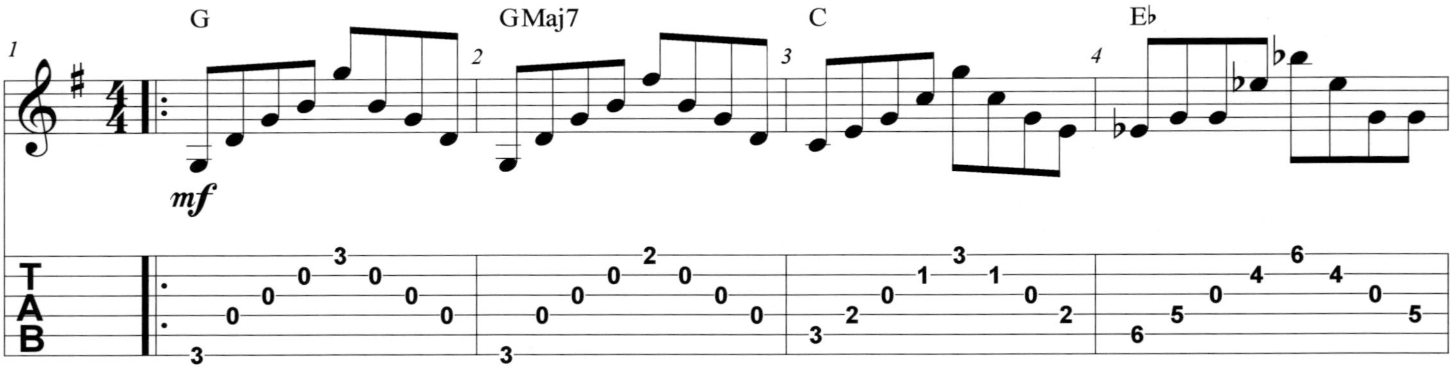

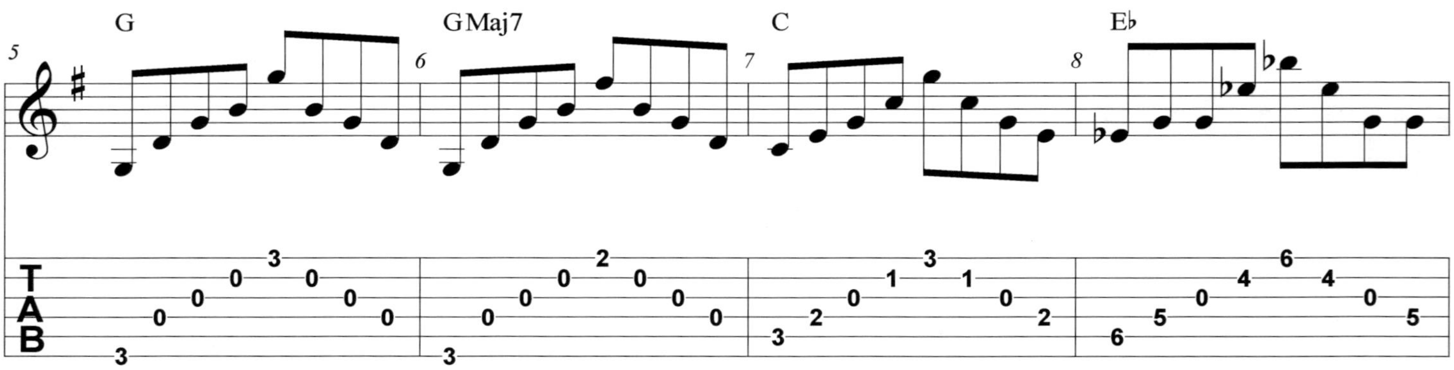

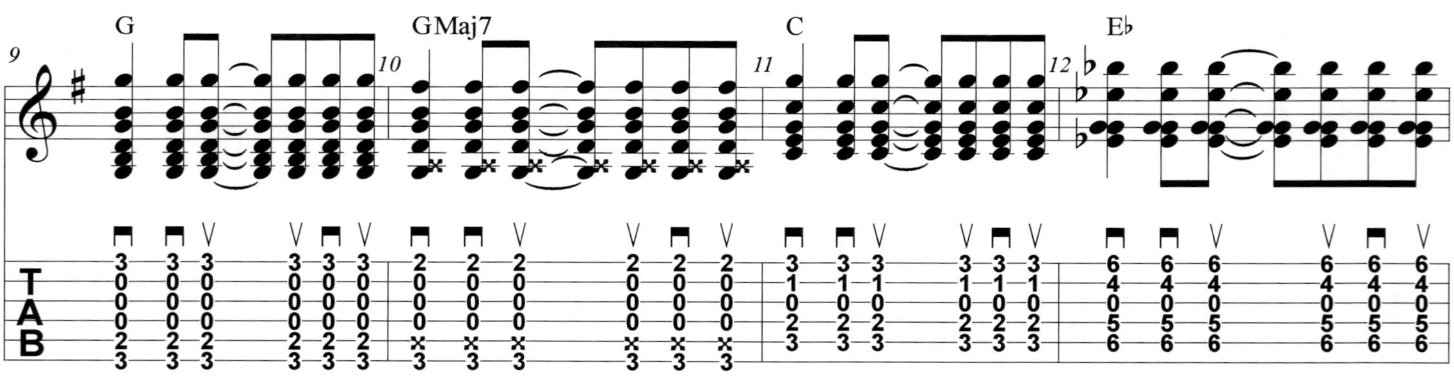

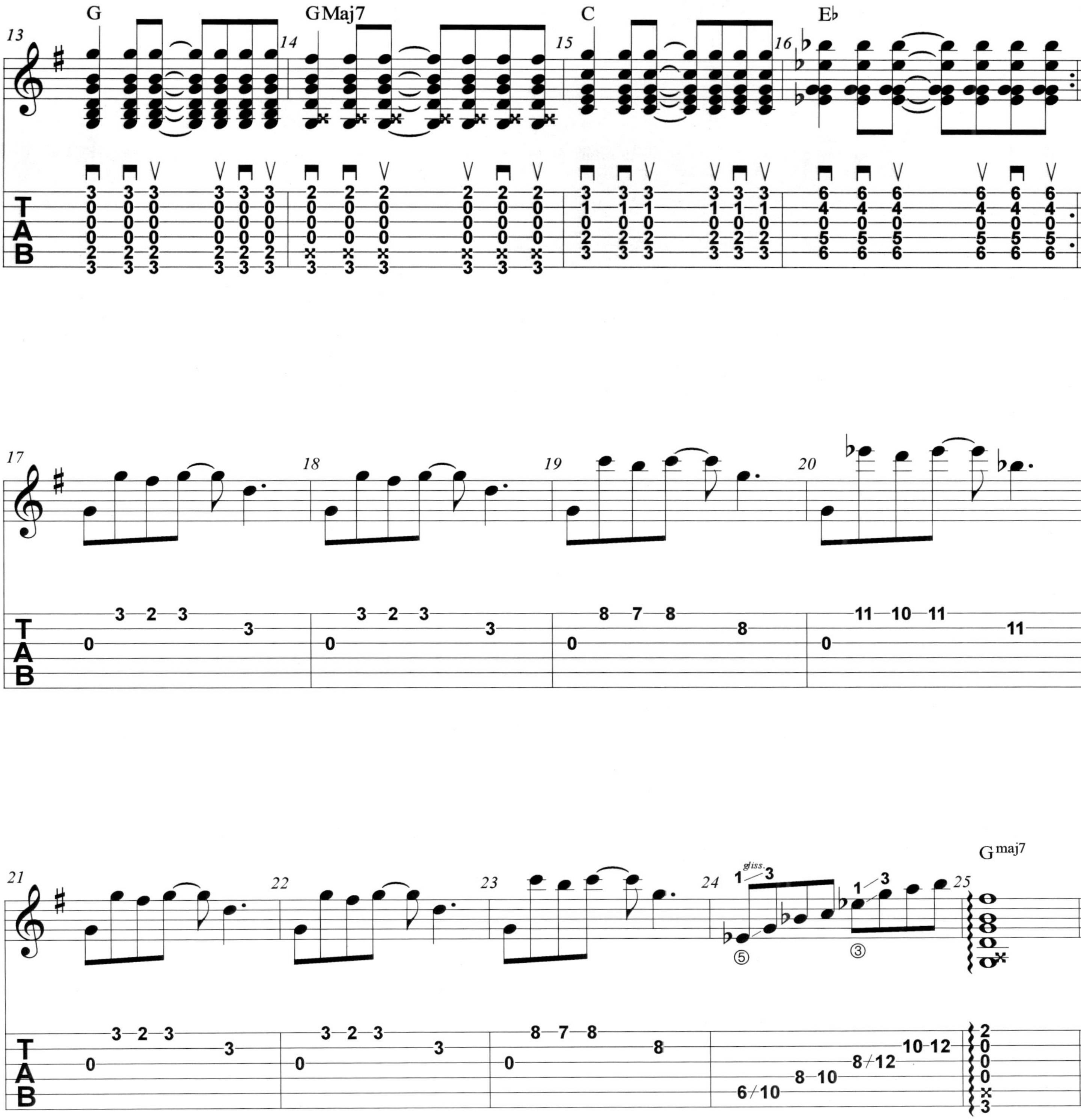
G
GMaj7
C
E♭
gliss.
Gmaj7

10

3rd-Finger Independence Etude

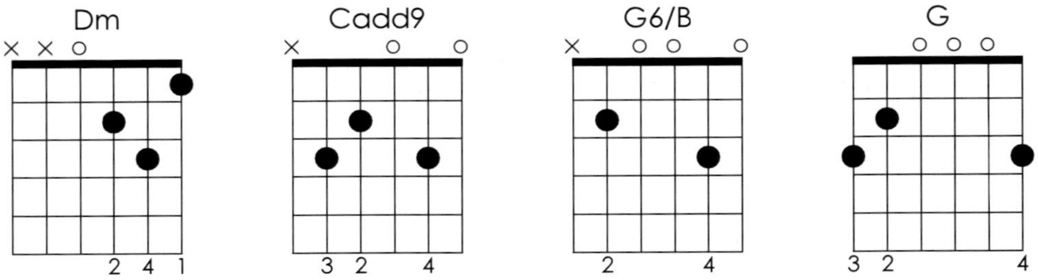

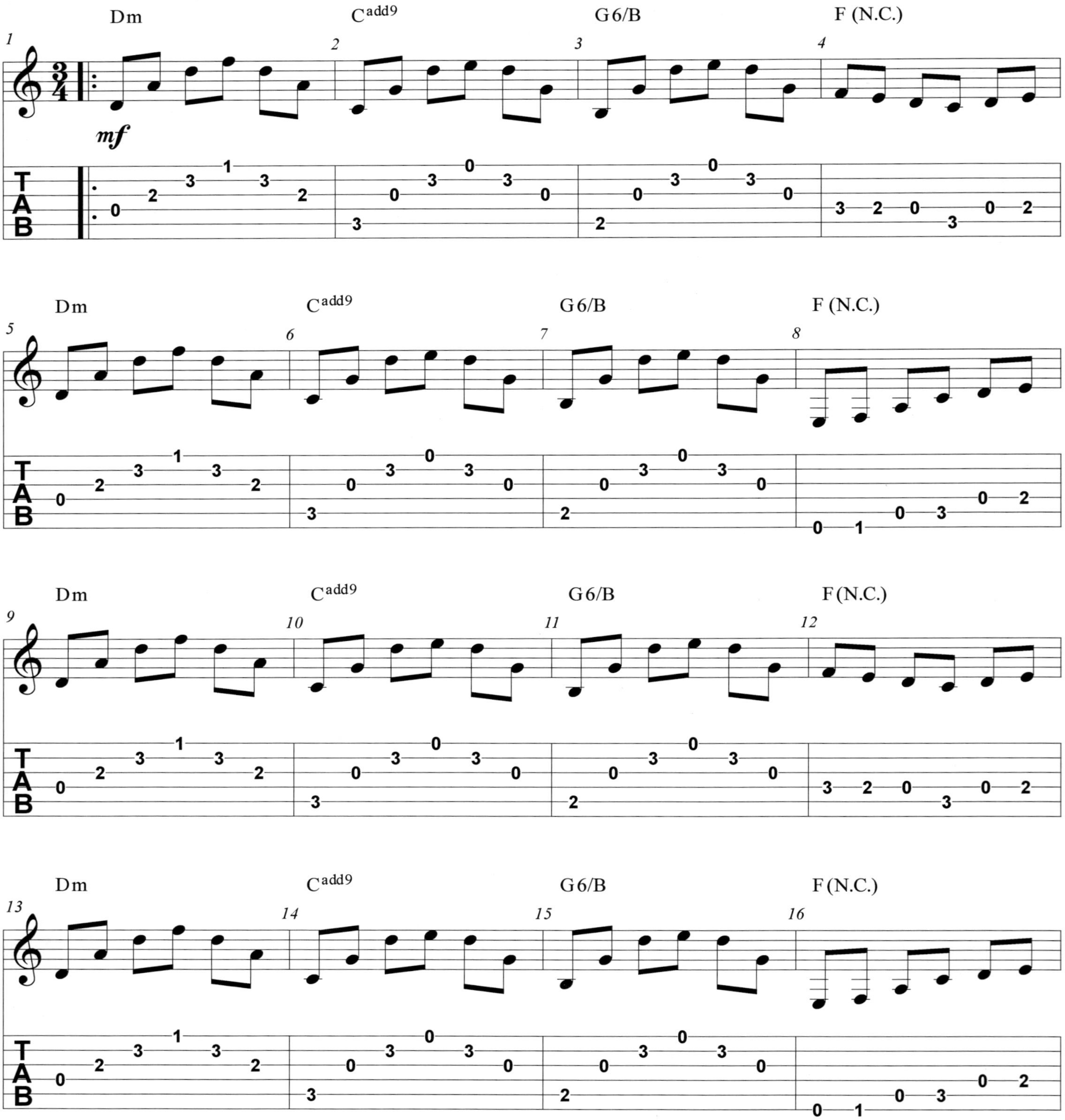

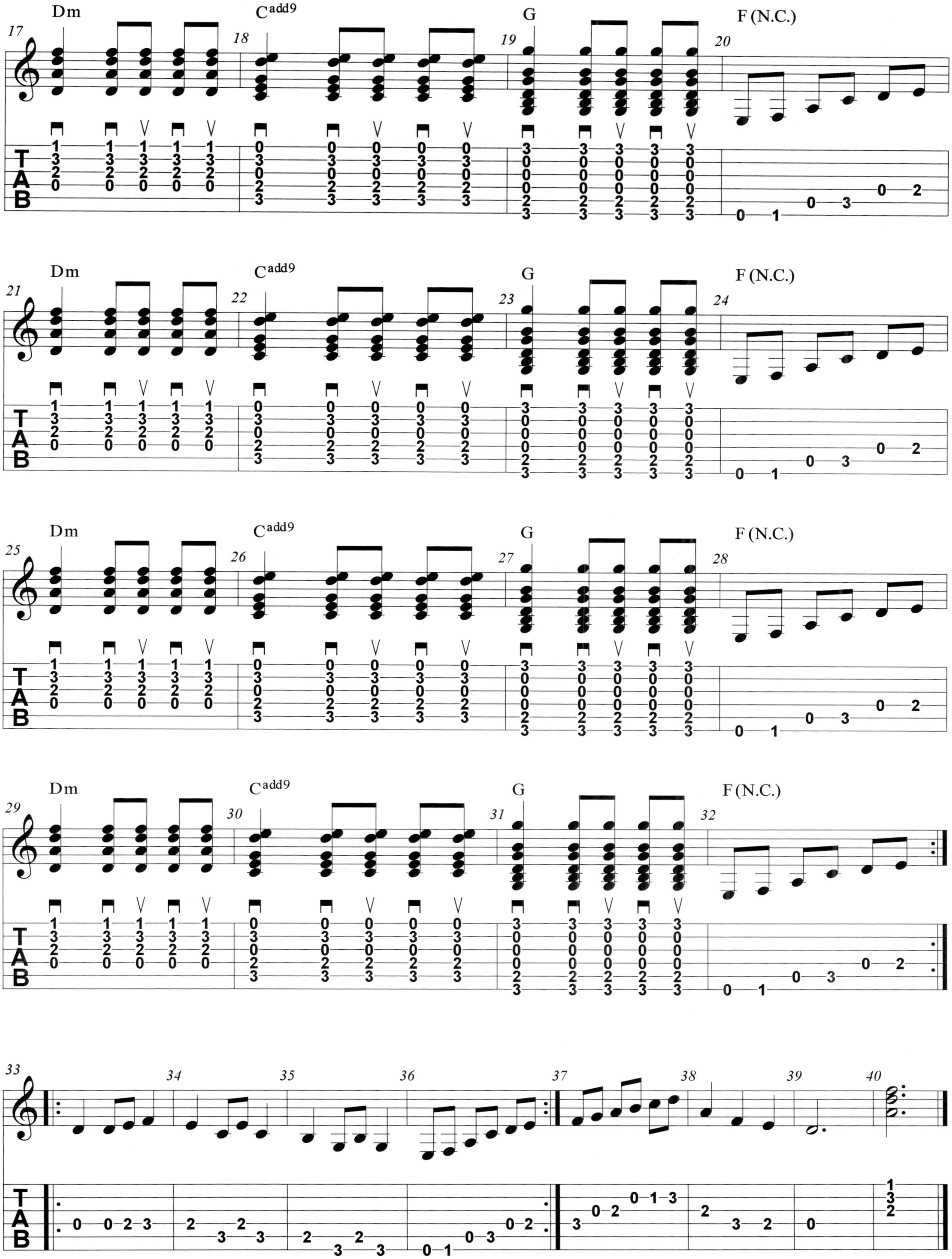
Dm
Cadd9
G
F (N.C.)

Hard Rock Etude #2

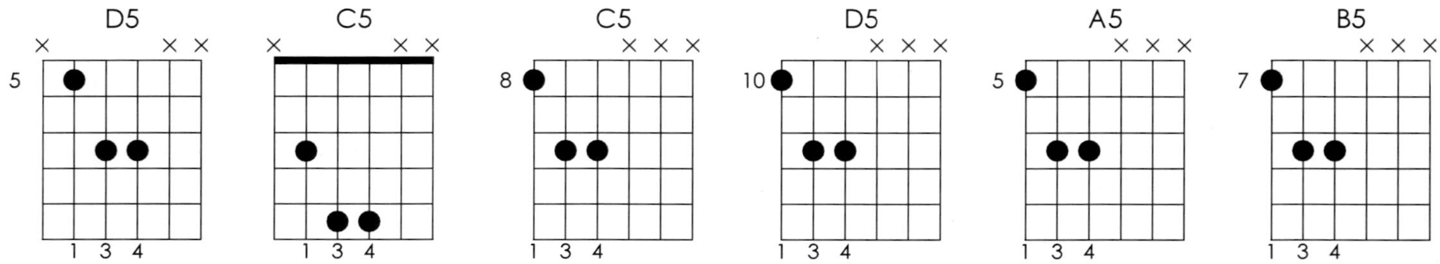

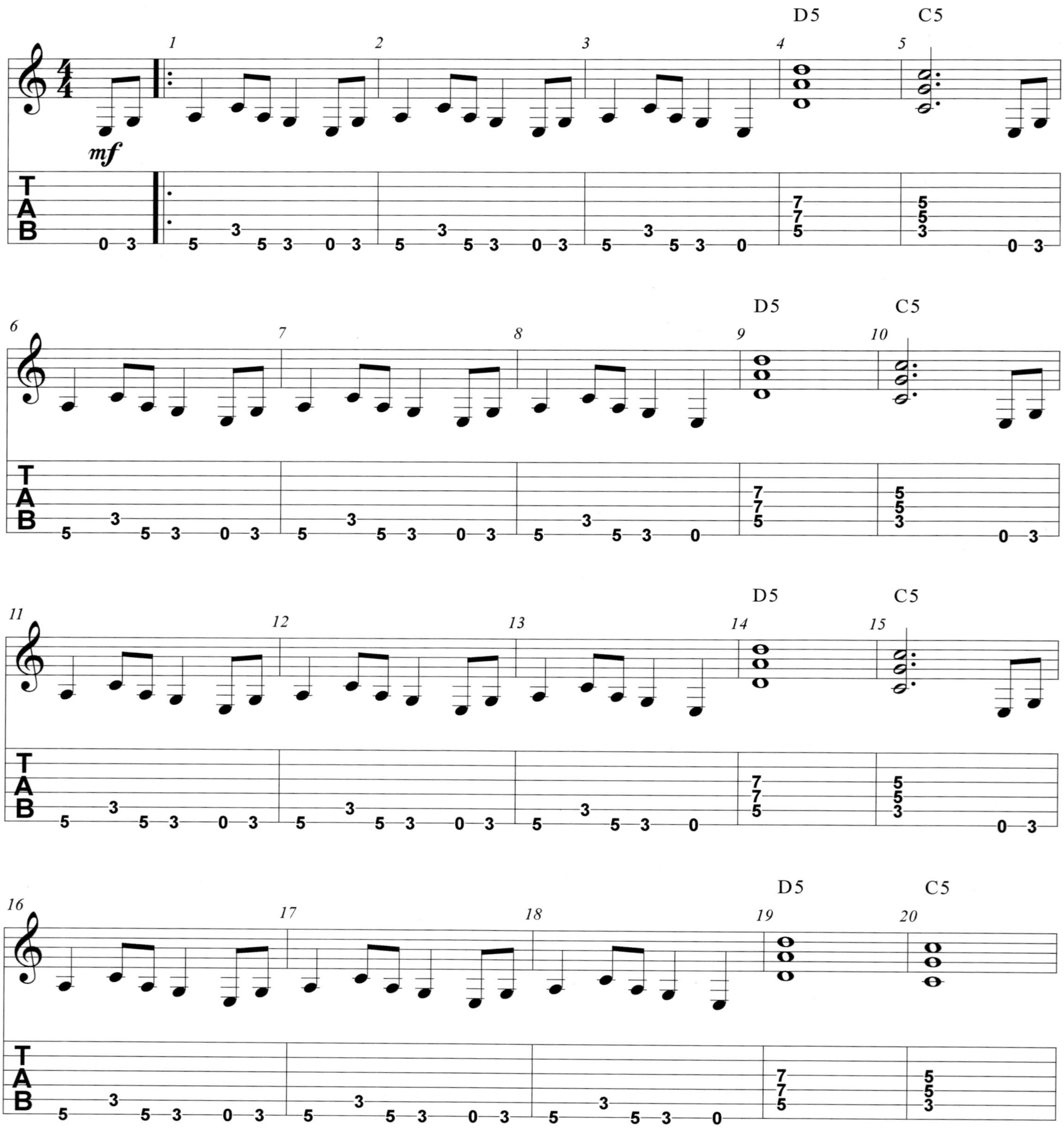

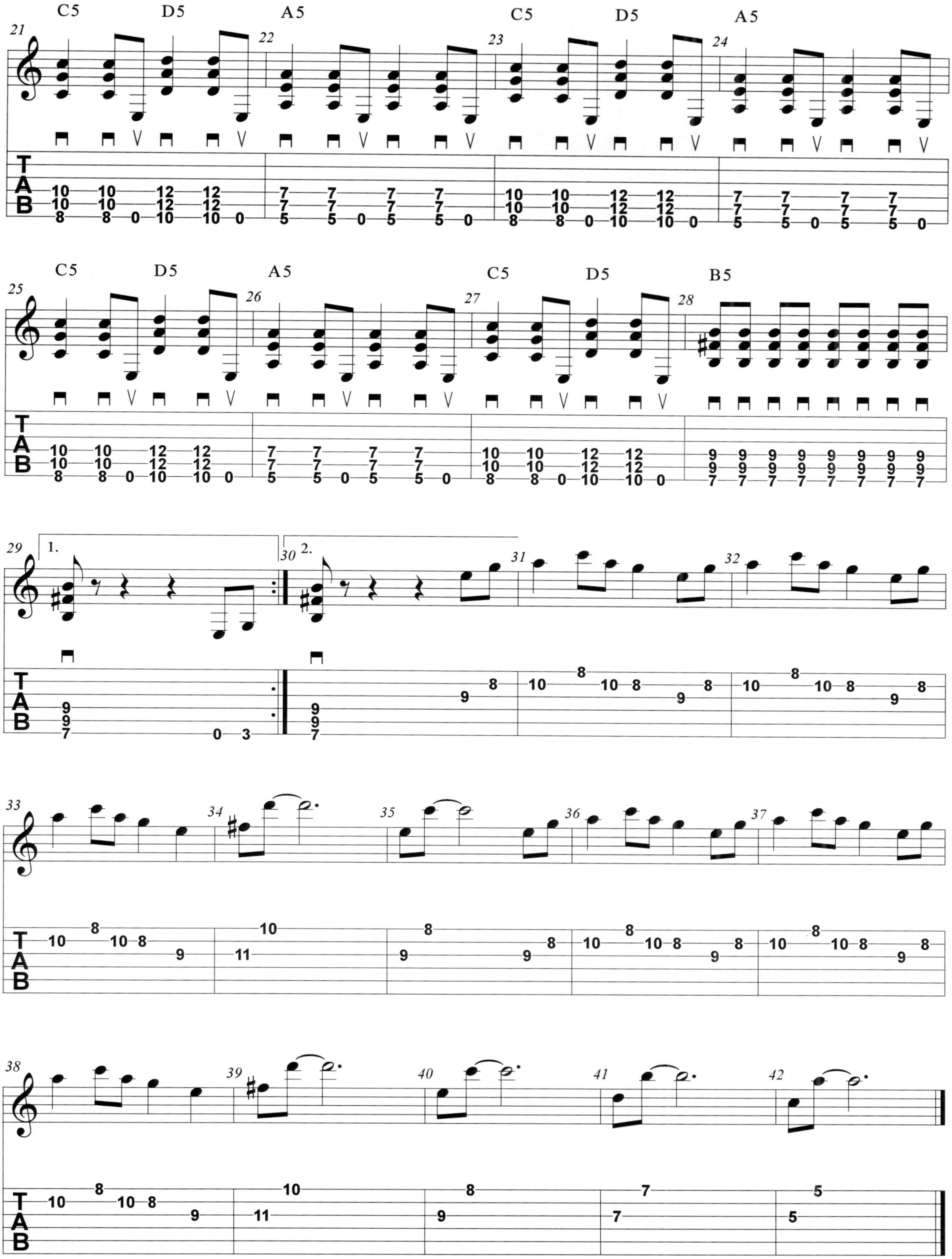
C5 D5 A5 C5 D5 A5
C5 D5 A5 C5 D5 B5
1.
2.
T
A
B

12

Descending Chord Tone Etude

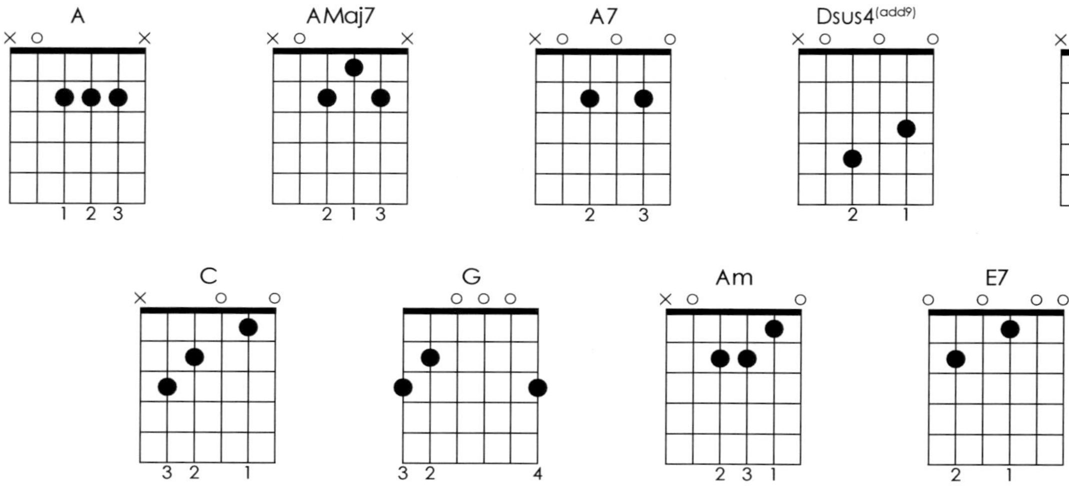

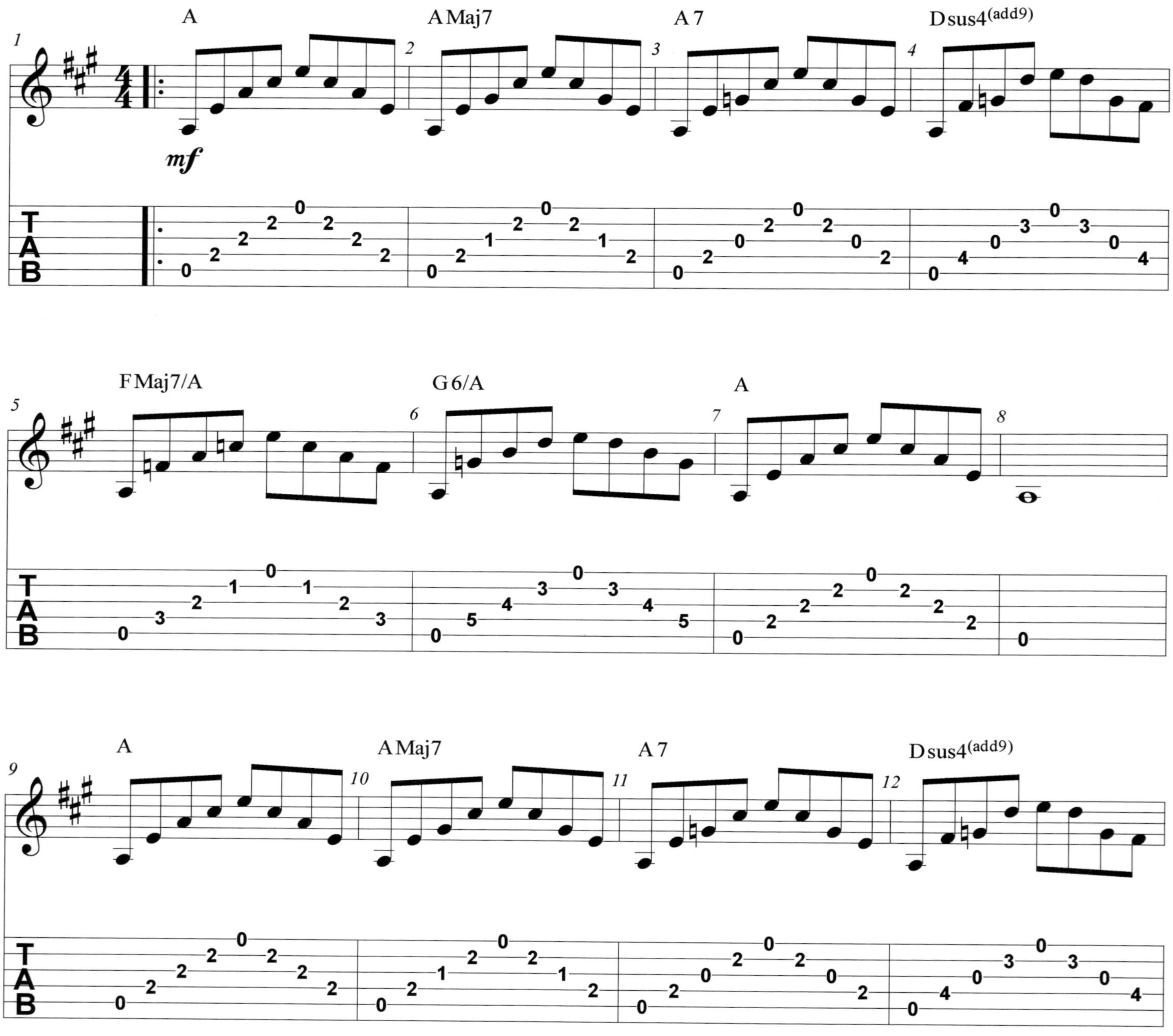

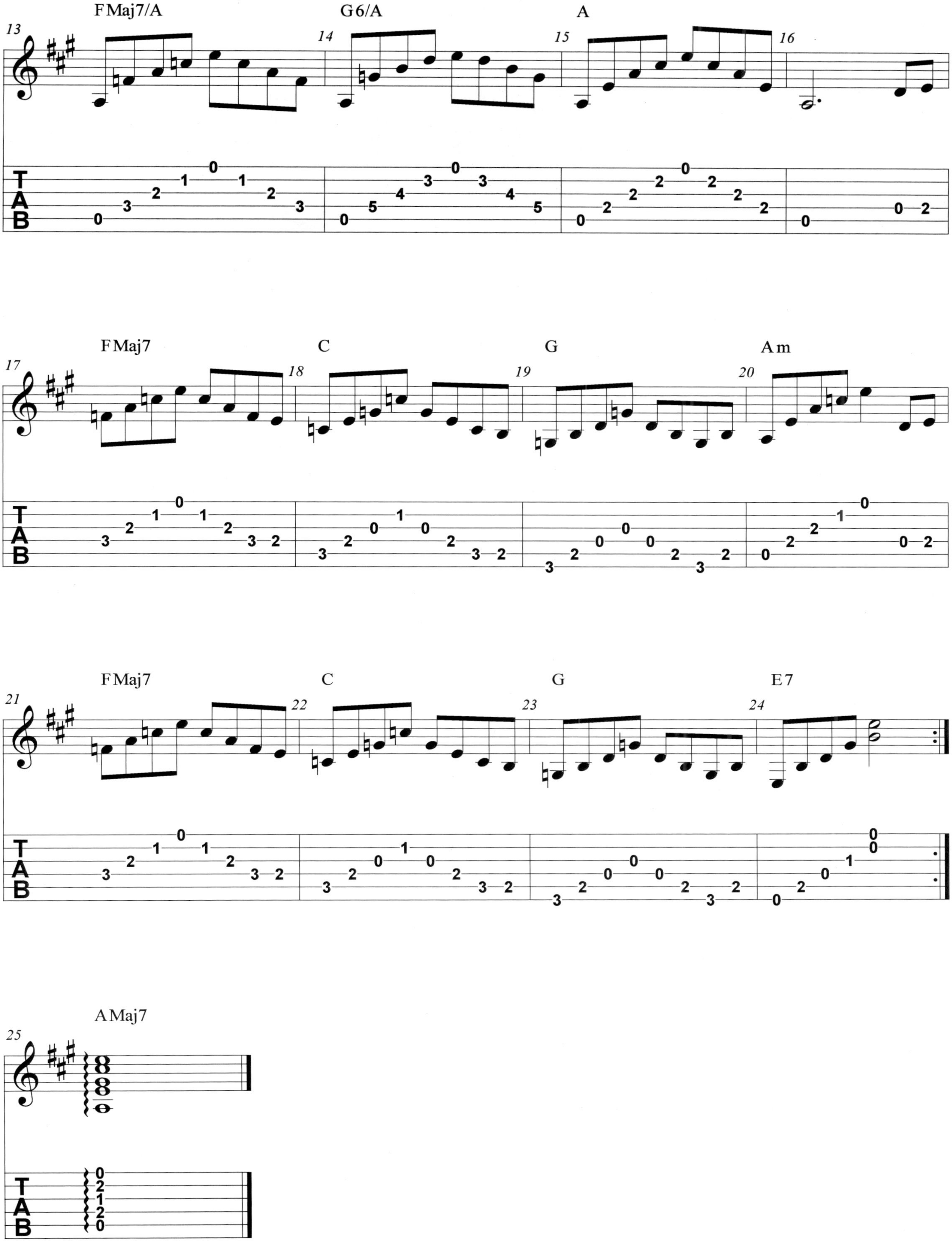
FMaj7/A
G6/A
A
FMaj7
C
G
Am
FMaj7
C
G
E7
AMaj7

13

D Minor Etude

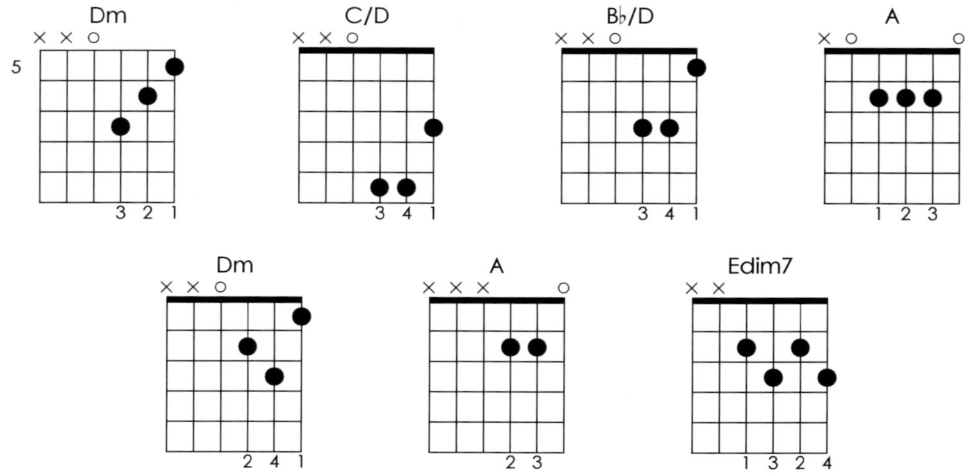

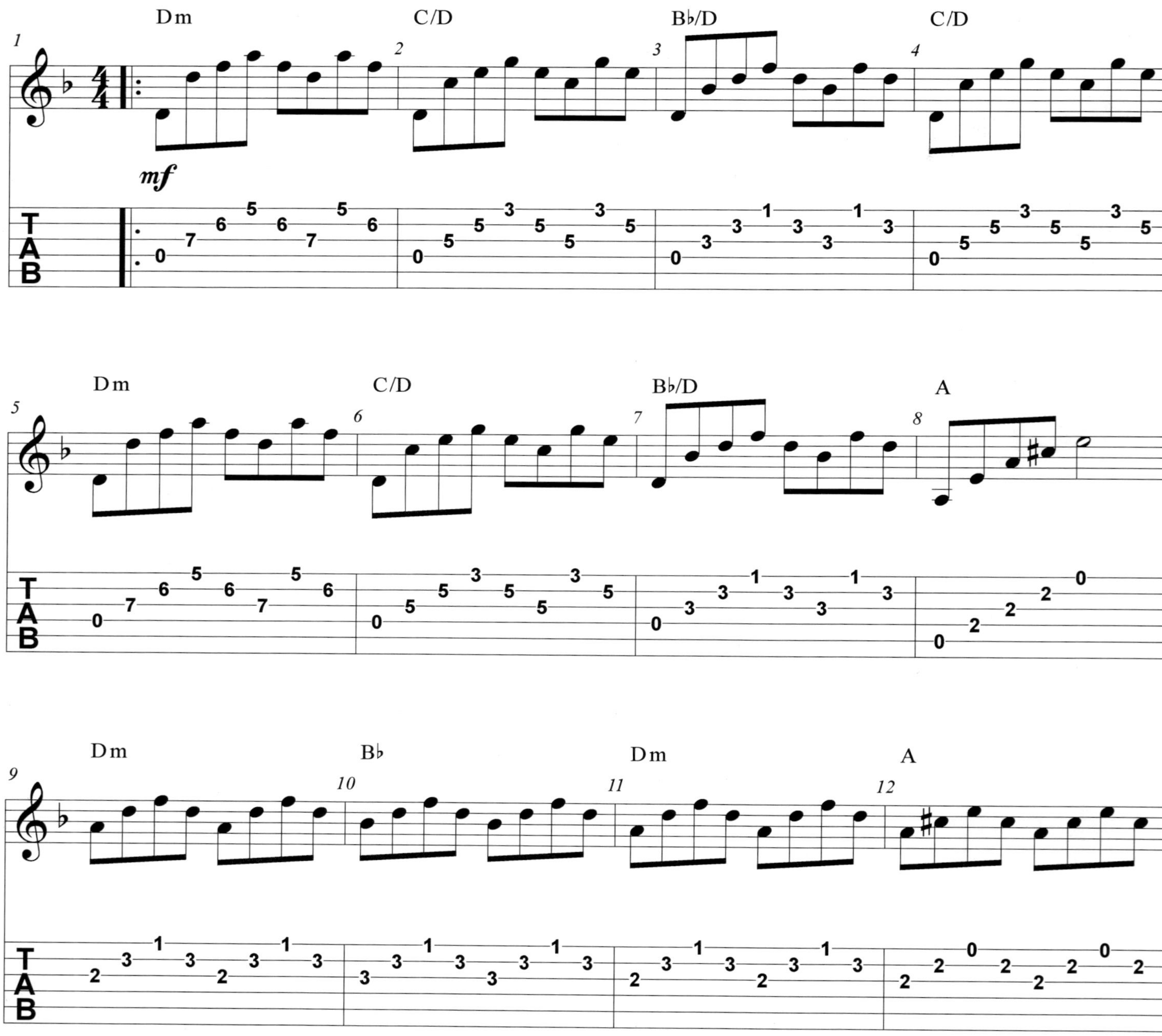

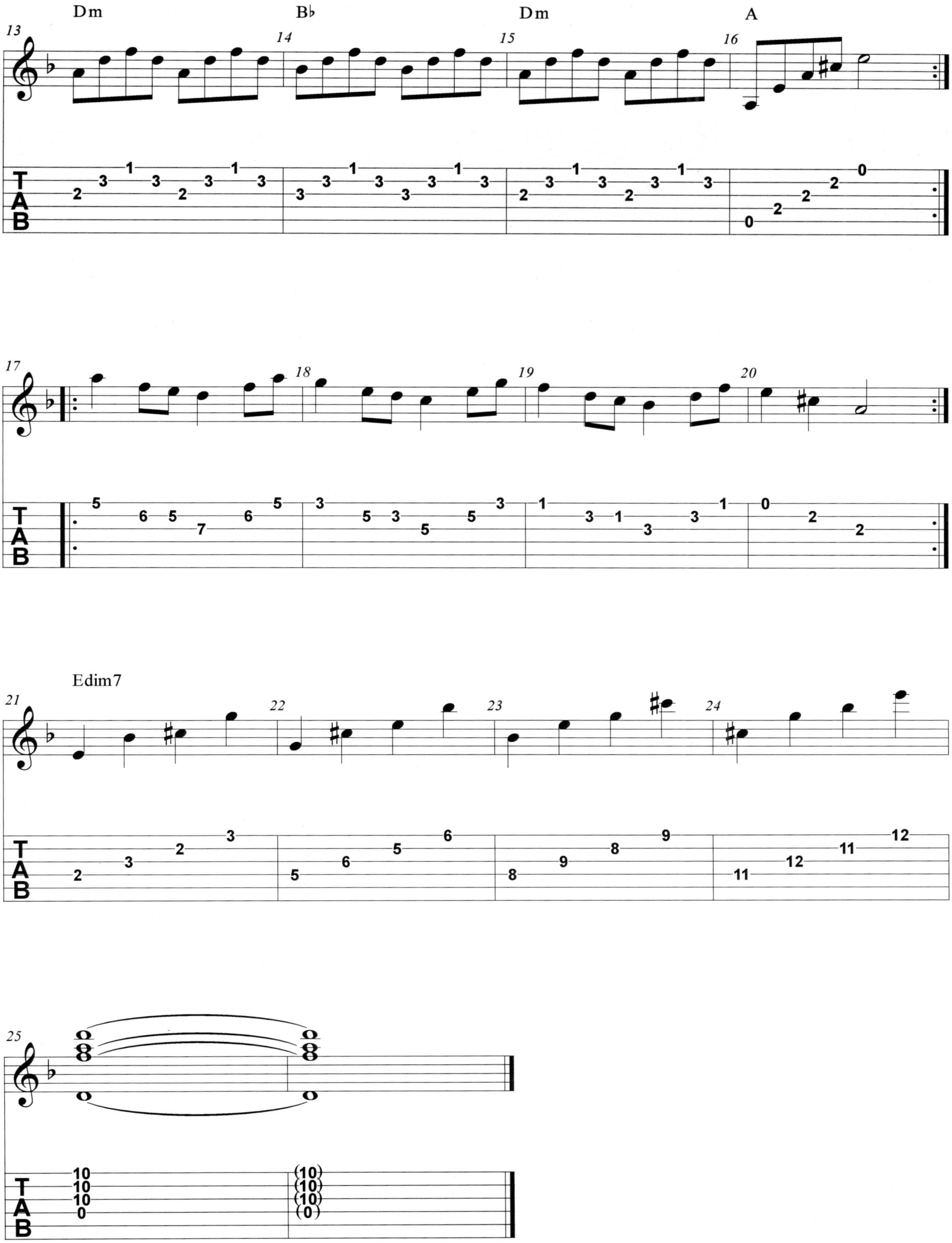
Dm
B♭
Dm
A
Edim7

About the Author

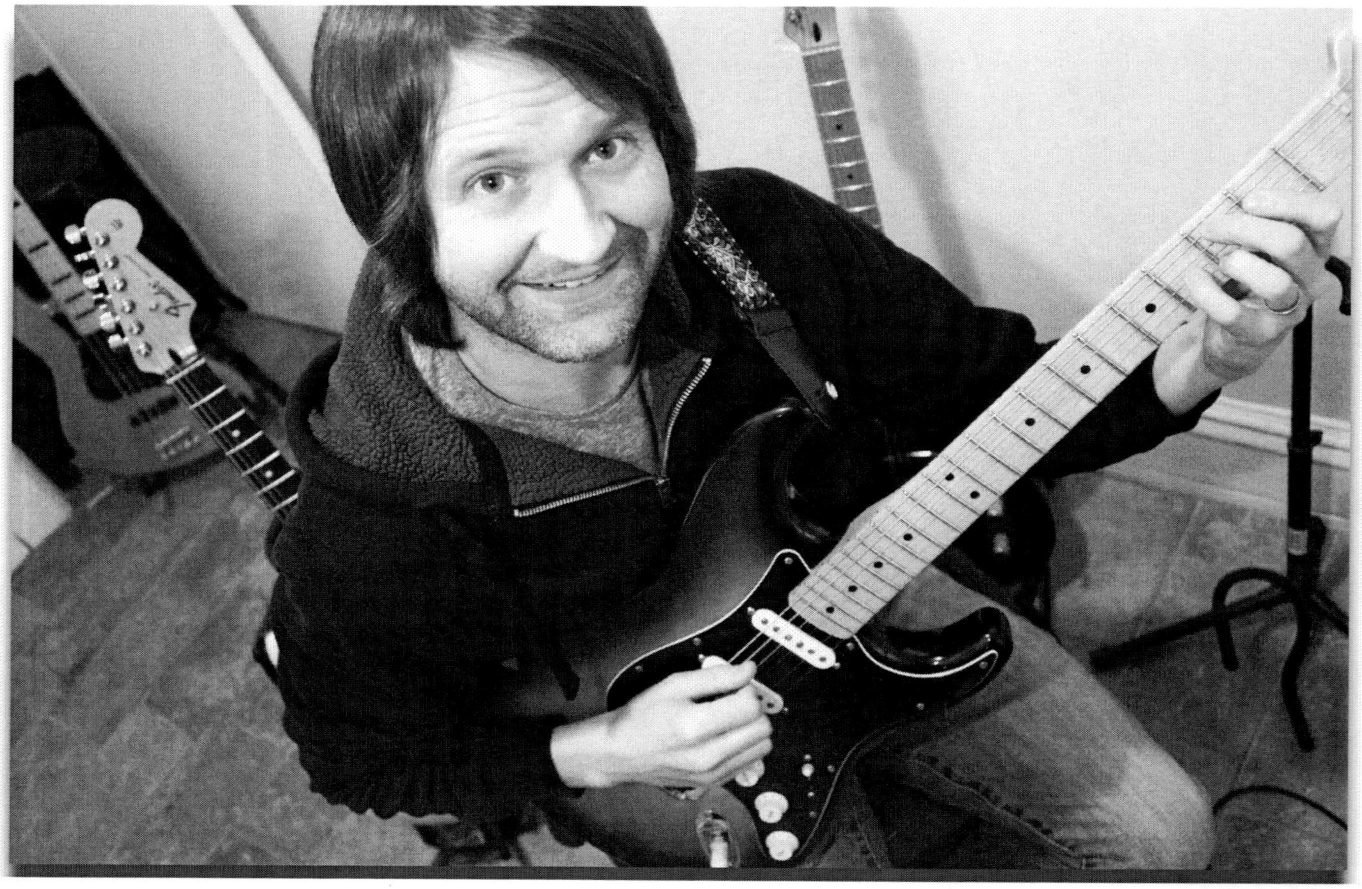

Adam Douglass

Adam Douglass has been performing professionally, composing and teaching since 2000. He currently resides in New York City. He has toured and performed as a guitarist with artists such as Tom Constanten (Grateful Dead, Jefferson Airplane), Charles Neville (The Neville Brothers) and many others. Currently performing in two eponymous bands, The Adam Douglass Triage performs his original music, while The Adam Douglass Trio performs jazz standards.

Notes

Other Mel Bay Rock and Contemporary Guitar Books

Advanced Modern Rock Guitar Improvisation (Finn)

Altered States (Delach)

Blues Jam Play-Along (W. Bay)

Blues/Rock Guitar Improvising (Finn)

Comping Styles for Funk (Arnold)

Complete Rock Guitar Book (M. Christiansen)

Easiest Rock Guitar Book (W. Bay)

Electric Blues Workout (Bowden)

Expanding Your Soloing (Reed)

Getting Into Rock Guitar (Delach)

Guitar Journals: Blues (Multiple Authors)

Guitar Journals: Rock (Multiple Authors)

Improvising Without Scales (Verheyen)

Playing the Blues: Blues Rhythm Guitar (Trovato/Stoubis)

MBGU Rock Curriculum: Fluid Soloing (Quinn)

MBGU Rock Curriculum: Foundations of Rock/Evolution of Rock Guitar (Driscoll)

MBGU Rock Curriculum: Foundations of Rock: Guitar Riffs in theStyle of the 60s & 70s (Finn)

MBGU Rock Curriculum: Foundations of Rock: Guitar Riffs in the Style of the 80s and 90s (Lappin)

MBGU Rock Curriculum: Rock Masterclass: 60 Tapping Licks (Anastassakis)

Rock Guitar Made Easy (C. Christiansen)

Rock Guitar Workout (Delach)

Rock/Fusion Improvising (Filipiak)

Rock Studies/Easy (Bull)